BELVIDERE

BELVIDERE

A Plantation Memory

COMMEMORATIVE EDITION

Anne Sinkler Fishburne

New Introduction by Anne Sinkler Whaley LeClercq

THE UNIVERSITY OF SOUTH CAROLINA PRESS

© 2015 University of South Carolina

Published by the University of South Carolina Press
Columbia, South Carolina 29208

www.sc.edu/uscpress

Manufactured in the United States of America

24 23 22 21 20 19 18 17 16 15
10 9 8 7 6 5 4 3 2 1

Library of Congress Cataloging-in-Publication Data
can be found at http://catalog.loc.gov/.

isbn: 978-1-61117-554-7 (paperback)
isbn: 978-1-61117-555-4 (ebook)

CONTENTS

Preface *ix*

Acknowledgments for the
Commemorative Edition *xi*

Introduction to the
Commemorative Edition *xiii*
Anne Sinkler Whaley LeClercq

Chapter 1	*1*
Chapter 2	*20*
Chapter 3	*33*
Chapter 4	*48*
Chapter 5	*61*
Chapter 6	*72*
Chapter 7	*80*
Chapter 8	*86*

Appendix: Abridged
Genealogical Table *93*

FOR

Emily Wharton Whaley, Anne Sinkler Whaley,
Martha Elizabeth Whaley, and Anne Moultrie Ball

PREFACE

It is not now as it hath been of yore—
  Turn whereso'er I may,
  By night or day,
The things which I have seen I now can see no more.

These familiar lines by Wordsworth could have been written especially for Belvidere, for most of the old place now lies beneath the muddy waters of Lake Marion. But though Belvidere is no more, the memories of many happy years remain. And so that Belvidere may live on and be known to succeeding generations, particularly to my granddaughters to whom this little book is dedicated, I have gathered together the letters and the memories which comprise this record.

I wish to express sincere gratitude to Mr. George Curry of the University of South Carolina's Department of History, who assisted in editing the material included in this book, and to Mr. Frank H. Wardlaw, Managing Editor of the University of South Carolina Press, who helped in many ways.

Thanks are also due to Mr. Henry Ravenel Dwight, "the Sage of St. John's," to Miss Catherine Cain of Pinopolis, and to Miss Anna Sinkler, formerly of Eutaw

Preface

plantation and now of Eutawville, for assistance with historical and genealogical data. Mrs. Jean Fleming of Charleston graciously granted permission for the reproduction of her water color of "The Street."

ANNE SINKLER FISHBURNE.

Pinopolis, S. C.
July, 1949

ACKNOWLEDGMENTS
for the
COMMEMORATIVE EDITION

Three persons have provided assistance as I prepared this introduction. They are Elizabeth Connor, former head of the Reference Department of the Daniel Library at the Citadel and now head of faculty development; Kevin Metzger, head of the museum and archives, Daniel Library; and Anne Moultrie Helms, who shared with me her collection of Belvidere Plantation guest books. All the illustrations that appear in this edition are from the 1949 edition of *Belvidere: A Plantation Memory* or are in my possession.

Anne Sinkler Whaley LeClercq

INTRODUCTION
to the
COMMEMORATIVE EDITION

Anne Sinkler Whaley LeClercq

MY GRANDMOTHER Anne (Nan) Wickham Sinkler Fishburne (1886–1981) was a lady of great courage, faith, and community spirit. She faced many challenges in life, but none was greater than dismantling her home on the Santee River, Belvidere Plantation, in the face of incipient destruction. She had known since 1938 that a New Deal–inspired combination of state and federal agencies, created and promoted by President Franklin Delano Roosevelt, U.S. Senator James F. Byrnes, and Governors Burnet Rhett Maybank and Richard Manning Jefferies of South Carolina, were determined to flood a portion of the Santee River basin to create Lakes Marion and Moultrie as sources for lowcountry hydroelectric power.[1] The plantation where she had grown up and that she farmed for her father, Charles St. George Sinkler (1853–1934), would be inundated.[2] All the residents of Belvidere, including African American families who had labored on the plantation for generations, would be displaced as Belvidere and its neighbors were submerged. Local churches and even the graves of those interred in nearby churchyards would have to be relocated to prevent their loss beneath the new lakes. Faced with this monumental challenge, she would have to denude

Belvidere's mansion of its furniture and strip its decorative mantels, doors, and doorframes, which would be given to friends and family. She also would help relocate the resident African American families from Belvidere to a new community that still exists today, Little Belvidere, on the outskirts of Eutawville.

Belvidere Plantation was situated among many neighboring plantations and farms on the Santee River in the old region known as Upper St. Johns Parish, South Carolina. The land was purchased in 1795 by Captain James Sinkler (1740–1800), a Scottish immigrant. Captain James first settled on a 1770 royal grant in St. Stephens Parish. He called this first plantation Old Santee. Freshets ruined their farming, so James and his brother Peter moved to St. John's Parish in 1790 and began growing cotton on the tract they named Belvidere. James's widow, Margaret Cantey Sinkler (1763–1821), built the Belvidere big house in 1805. Their son, William Sinkler (1787–1853), known as the "beau-père," established nearby Eutaw Plantation in 1809. The two plantations were separated by Eutaw Creek, a clear stream that sprung Arethusa-like from Eutaw Springs. The Belvidere and Eutaw plantations provided their owners great fortunes from raising short-staple cotton. In one year Belvidere produced 216 pounds of cotton per acre, selling the crop for seventy-five cents a pound.[3] In April 1861 Belvidere's inhabitants heard the cannon fire as Confederates bombarded Fort Sumter, sixty-five miles away in Charleston Harbor, sounds that signaled the start of the Civil War. The dull glow of the western sky would later bring to mind Union general William T. Sherman's path of destruction through the defeated state.

Belvidere was a two-story timber house with four rooms on each floor. A brick staircase with curved brick banisters led up to a covered porch where everyone gathered during the day to read, sew, and

Introduction to the Commemorative Edition

tell stories. On the left side of the front porch, a door led into the dining room with a fireplace. There was a pantry off of the dining room. The kitchen was an outbuilding with its own side entrance into the pantry. On the right side of the porch, a door led into the parlor that also had a fireplace. Off of the parlor was a bedroom. On the back side of the first floor, there was a laundry. Stairs led to the second floor and into an expansive hall. Nan's parents, Anne Wickham Porcher Sinkler (1860–1919) and Charles St. George Sinkler (1853–1934), had a big bedroom on the second floor, and off their bedroom was the nursery. A guest bedroom and Caroline (Carrie) Sidney Sinkler's bedroom completed the second floor. Carrie (1894–1993) was Nan's younger sister, named after her father's sister Caroline Sidney Sinkler (1860–1949). Stretching behind the Belvidere house were a smokehouse and Maum Rosena and Daddy Lewis DeSaussure's cabin, and beyond that the "street" of cabins that were homes to more than 150 African American descendants of Sinkler family slaves.[4] Belvidere bordered Eutawville, a pineland village, and was surrounded by several other Santee River plantations. Across Eutaw Springs were Eutaw Plantation, with its historical marker on the Revolutionary War battlefield; Thomas Porcher's Walworth; Walnut Grove; Pond Bluff; Oaklands; and Mountain Hope. Access to the plantations was provided by S.C. Highway 46, the Atlantic Coast Line Railroad that crossed the Santee River between the Black Jack and Dorshee plantations, and the navigable waters of the Santee.

Because Belvidere was rather isolated, friends and family visiting for holidays often spent several days or weeks. During Christmas and Easter seasons, the house was filled to capacity. Nan recalled wonderful, long visits from Uncle Wharton Sinkler (1845–1910), "Aunty" Elizabeth Allen Sinkler (1843–1916), and "Aunt Cad,"

Introduction to the Commemorative Edition

Caroline Sidney Sinkler. Uncle Wharton, a distinguished Philadelphia physician, came down in the fall to hunt, bringing friends and hunting dogs. Nan told delightful stories of his hunting escapades. Elizabeth and Cad visited every Easter, bringing new dresses and hats for their nieces Nan, Em, and Carrie. The house was polished to the nines, with food prepared and warm welcomes ready for family and friends.

Uncle Wharton and Aunty died in 1910 and 1916, respectively, but Aunt Cad visited Belvidere every year until the plantation ceased to exist. Special trips were planned for her to family-owned plantations. Nan's account of their visit to Gippy Plantation on the Cooper River, purchased in 1927 by her sister Emily and her husband, Nicholas Guy Roosevelt (1883–1965), is poetic.

> The drive through the swamp was lovely, for the afternoon sun shining through the green leaves which canopied the road gave a luminous light as though we were under water. Suddenly from this subdued light, we came out into the brilliant sunshine and there stretched before us were the rice fields with their flocks of chattering red-winged blackbirds and little marsh wrens swinging back and forth on the slender reeds."[5]

As was the custom of the day, Belvidere kept guest books, or registers, in which visitors recorded their names and impressions—even artistic sketches—of their sojourns. Christmas and Easter were the busiest celebrations, but there were always guests at Belvidere enjoying hunting and riding. Two surviving guest books record the names and memories of family and friends who visited the plantation. The first of these two begins with a Swedish toast by Eckley B. Coxe, Jr. (1872–1916), on April 8, 1901: "Ein Skoal! Dein Skoal! Alla

Introduction to the Commemorative Edition

valla fleckros Skoal!" (To my health! To your health! To the health of all pretty girls!). Other notes captured the household's charm and gaiety. Caroline Sidney Sinkler wrote, "Here's where my heart is turning ever." On March 21, 1901, Charlie Sinkler observed, "At the outset I desire to extol the Southern hospitality so justly widely famous and to express the belief that it has achieved its perfection at Belvidere. The charm of the plantation may be subtle but it is undoubtedly irresistible, and I am proud to acknowledge being entirely dominated by it." On November 26, 1901, William Sinkler wrote, "Guns and Dogs, Men and Togs, Quick mules, Old fools, Hat stands, bene bands, clash eats, ned beats; Some times, Are divine, Generalissimos, To the Nose, Scottish Chiefs, Brings no Grief, Ever near, Belvidere." Callen Jones Jervey observed on December 26, 1901: "I always shall Remember, Those days of youthful fun, We spent at dear old Belvidere, At Xmas '01."

During the same Christmas season, Harriott C. Williams noted, "Belvidere, a Paradise on earth." On January 8, 1902, S. E. Porcher of El Paso, Texas, indicated: "Oh! How good it is to be; Again once more in old S.C.: The West has sheltered us awhile; And I have come o'er many a mile; To find a welcome sweet and true; Warming my heart all through and through; And what delight it is to share; The gracious charms of Belvidere."[6]

A second guest book dates from 1916 to 1939. On January 30, 1916, Richard and Elizabeth A. Manning wrote, "Where e'er I roam, whatever realms I see, My heart untraveled fondly turns to thee." The April 15, 1916, marriage of Emily Wharton Sinkler to Nicholas Guy Roosevelt was recorded with the names of the wedding party. Nan was sick at the time, so she recounted the wedding through the eyes of her sister Carrie, as related in a letter from her.

Introduction to the Commemorative Edition

Well here it is, the big moment! And you can picture the lawn bathed in soft April sunshine, the old cedars casting their long shadows. An aisle opened up between the guests from the front steps to the big live oak, and there was Bishop Guerry, benign and imposing in the enormous white muslin sleeves and robes of his office, and Mother walking down on Cousin Richard's arm to take her place.[7]

Two future giants of South Carolina literature visited Belvidere in the winter of 1917. In a poignant, prescient entry of January 5, 1917, the twenty-two-year-old Josephine Lyons Scott Pinckney wrote:

And peace upon your pasture lands I found,
Where grazing flocks drift on continually,
As little clouds that travel with no sound,
Across a windless sky.
Out of your oaks the birds call to their mates,
That brood among the pines,
Where hidden deep,
From curious eyes a world's adventure waits,
In columned choirs of sleep.
I sing of peace.
Was it but yesterday I came among your roses and your Bees?
Then momentarily amid this wrath I pray for yesterday reborn.

Dubose Heyward stayed at Belvidere during January 1917 and wrote in the guest book:

Come tell me: when the nation has gone dry.
And you are standing with your final glass, Pressed to your lips;

Introduction to the Commemorative Edition

When mingled with your sigh,
You breathe one toast more tender then the rest,
That in its measure holds them all comprest;
Come, will it be to Fortune, or a lass?
Oh, I will drink to Springtime and to Youth,
And hearts that harbor April all the year.
To dancing eyes and laughter;
And in truth to many cheery welcomes I have met,
That found my heart and caused it to forget,
The thousand cares that stalk this dismal sphere.
And I will add the golden,
Misty glow of yellow jasmine,
When the evening's clear,
And one old fashioned garden that I know,
Where trellised bloom is framing tender skies.
All there, and more,
I'll mingle with my sighs,
Then drink one long, deep toast to Belvidere.

Saint Patrick's Day, March 17, 1918, bore a wartime entry of Frederic LeClercq, U.S. Naval Reserve Forces, the uncle of my husband, Fred. Josephine Pinckney and Emily Wharton Roosevelt were back at Belvidere on January 15, 1920. Anne W. Fishburne and W. Kershaw Fishburne signed the guest book with many others on Christmas 1921. In 1923 Josephine Pinckney and Mary Fanning Wickham Porcher of Chestnut Hill, Philadelphia, were visiting. At Thanksgiving 1930, my mother and aunt signed their names: Emily Wharton Fishburne and Anne Sinkler Fishburne. Josephine Pinckney and Dunbar Lockwood were guests from February 23 to March 13, 1931. An inscription recorded on Easter Sunday 1937

Introduction to the Commemorative Edition

documents one of Nan's most public accomplishments at Belvidere, reviving horse racing among the Eutawville plantations: "Lovely peaceful sunny days and moonlit nights and on Saturday a brilliant gala day of the Races." As must all things, the Belvidere guest book ended, with its last entry made on March 31, 1939: Augustine T. Smythe, Jr.'s fateful statement, "After us the Deluge."[8]

Nan was courageous and resourceful. Family legend has it that Nan had fallen in love with a young country doctor, William Kershaw Fishburne (1880–1968). Nan's mother, Anne Wickham Porcher Sinkler, disapproved of the romance and—in time-honored manner—sought to discourage her daughter by sending her abroad. Anne arranged with her sister Lizzie Coxe for Nan to be taken out of the country for five months. Nan accompanied Aunty on a trip to Istanbul in 1910, but the grand plan was unsuccessful.[9] My female forebears reported that Nan returned to the United States and fell off the train at Branchville into the arms of Kershaw Fishburne.[10] They were married on April 14, 1910.

Weddings were more often celebratory occasions for the Sinklers at Belvidere. Nan's two first cousins, Laura Ann Stevens and Elizabeth Allen Stevens, had moved in 1904 from Northampton, a cotton plantation in Upper St. Johns, to Lewisfield, a rice plantation on the Cooper River. The trip between the cousins was now a thirty-four-mile journey over dirt roads. Nan described the wedding of Elizabeth Stevens to Alexander Martin of Virginia as "one of the greatest events of my girlhood."[11] The Belvidere household, white and black, headed to Lewisfield in a procession of carts and carriages. The bridesmaids wore white net dresses and satin slips Aunty Lizzie had brought from Philadelphia. The grand wedding took place in the Lewisfield house, and the dancing lasted into the next morning.

Introduction to the Commemorative Edition

When Nan married Dr. Fishburne, she moved with him to Pinopolis, South Carolina. The Pinopolis house was built in 1914 near the Ophir Plantation summerhouse. Ophir was another of the plantations submerged by Lake Moultrie and the Santee Cooper power and navigation project. Nan sketched in the sand the house she wanted built, which had a close resemblance to Belvidere, with its curving brick staircase. She then went to Pennsylvania for the summer to stay with Aunt Elizabeth Sinkler Coxe. When Nan returned in August to Pinopolis, her lovely house—which turned one hundred years old in 2014—had been completed. Nan lived there until her death in 1981.[12]

William Kershaw Fishburne was a magnetic, wonderful man. My grandmother's constant challenge was to let her husband follow his path as a country doctor and to set her personal compass in a direction that would keep them busy and fulfilled. For example, Doc—as we all called him—had his inside dogs, Prince and Traveler, as well as forty-two beagles and hound dogs in the yard. Louisa Johnson, a cook nicknamed "Babe," fixed those dogs huge pots of boiled stew, which they ate with gusto. Nan and Doc filled their Pinopolis yard with horses because they both loved to ride. Doc built a tennis court and taught their daughters, Emily Fishburne Whaley and Anne Sinkler Ball, how to play. He was an excellent tennis player.

Nan was a true community spirit. She began the Pinopolis lancing tournament in 1955 to raise money for the town's Trinity Episcopal Church and to beautify its streets. This tournament brought hundreds of visitors to Gippy, the plantation home of her sister Emily Roosevelt and her husband, Nicholas. It was held in the spring of each year under Gippy's towering oaks. The lancing tournament carried on a tradition of horsemanship and chivalry that Nan had revived at Belvidere. Two decades earlier, in 1936, she had reorganized the St. John's Jockey Club and created a racecourse at Belvidere. The club, track, and racing tradition were sadly short-lived. Within three years the task of dismantling Belvidere was underway. Photographs from the first race revealed all the excitement of the day from weighing in the jockeys, close finishes, and black jockeys racing on mules, as well as capturing Anne Sinkler Fishburne and Carrie Sinkler Lockwood enjoying the fun-filled day.

My cousin Sidney Lockwood Tynan informed me that she had attended the final race season in spring 1939 and "that the Charleston bookies were amazed to see all the plantation horses winning and beating the Charleston thoroughbreds." Unfortunately the track and Belvidere lay in the flood path of the Santee Cooper project. In 1941 the house was emptied, and the family left the property for the last time. The racetrack is now underwater.

CHARLES SINKLER AND Emily Wharton Sinkler, Nan's grandparents, were married in 1842 and lived first at Eutaw Plantation and then moved into Belvidere in 1848, where they restored the house and garden. Emily and Charles had five children: Elizabeth Allen Sinkler (1843–1916), Wharton Sinkler (1845–1910), Charles St. George Sinkler (1853–1934), Mary Wharton Sinkler (1857–1934), and Caroline Sidney Sinkler (1860–1949). In *Belvidere: A Plantation Memory*, the plantation story is related partly through Emily Wharton's letters to her father, Thomas Isaac Wharton, of Philadelphia (1791–1856). Emily recounted the carriage rides, the hunting parties, and the musical evenings. She also described the fear of yellow fever that drove them from the plantation during the "sickly season." Having restored the garden at Belvidere, Emily took particular delight was her rose garden, filled with such varieties as the Glory of

France, Groille, Harrisonian de Brunnius, Cloth of Gold, and Souvenir de Malmaison.[13] Nan had known and loved her grandfather Charles Sinkler, who helped raise her at Belvidere Plantation.

Nan's parents, Charles St. George Sinkler and Anne (Annie) Wickham Porcher Sinkler (1860–1919), wed in 1883. Charles and Annie had first met that same year in Eutawville when Annie returned from New York City, where she had been raised after the Civil War. Annie was visiting her grandfather Thomas Porcher of Walworth Plantation.[14] At home Miss Annie was much loved by the African Americans living nearby because she ministered to their social and medical well-being. She once mixed pitchers of peppermint, asafetida, paregoric, and soda when there was an epidemic of "stomach complaint," and she also led Bible classes.[15]

Born in 1886, Nan was named for her mother. She was raised in the rural setting of an old plantation house, where she learned to cook, sew, play the piano, and ride horses, and also where she read the poetry of Alfred, Lord Tennyson, and the tales of Henry Wadsworth Longfellow. A true denizen of Upper St. John's Parish, she was grounded in the earth, sky, and livelihood of Belvidere. Nan fondly described growing up at Belvidere. She recalled with particular affection Maum Hetty's "gator stew" and pots of collards and how Maum Ellen churned milk into butter. "Daddy Duck Peter" was Charles Sinkler's plantation foreman. "Daddy Major" gave sermons that were accompanied by much shouting and singing, and he also smoked hams after November's "killing time." Nan perceived the lives of "plantation Negroes" as carefree and secure.

The relationship of landowner and tenant was that of mutual dependence and satisfaction. The wheels of plantation life were kept turning by the African American population; its profitable operation was possible only with their labor. On the other hand, the tenants'

Introduction to the Commemorative Edition

rent-free housing was kept in good repair, garden land and housing for livestock were also free, and work was always available to the tenants at fair wages.[16]

The sixty-six years that have passed between the first 1949 edition of *Belvidere* and this commemorative edition have witnessed a revolution in understanding the history and sociology of the South and the powerful impact of memory on historical perceptions. These progressive changes plus the need for all voices of the past to be documented—especially those of black South Carolinians—surely alter our perception of events as opposed to Nan's own view. No doubt not all the questions raised by older publications such as *Belvidere* have been asked and answered. What revelations will the next era experience?

Nan was not just a plantation girl. She had traveled with her aunt Lizzie Coxe all over the world: Istanbul, Alexandria, Venice, Rome, Vienna, Paris, and London. Some of Nan's travels with her aunt and her sister Emily and first cousins Laura and Elizabeth Stevens are told in *Elizabeth Sinkler Coxe's Tales from the Grand Tour, 1890–1910*.

As was customary, Nan kept scrapbooks. One of them was her account of a June 1934 trip to Great Britain and Europe with her cousin Margaret Day on the SS *Champlain*, a French ocean liner under the command of Captain Victor Barthelemy. Nan began this scrapbook with a Western Union telegram from her father and sister: "Have a swell time; take care of yourself; love." Arriving in London, they rented a Morris Minor automobile, and Nan obtained a European driver's license, number 4284, on June 11, 1934. The cost of the car rental was twelve pounds. Nan and Peggy headed out for Ely in Cambridgeshire and stayed in the Lamb Hotel; while in the area, they visited the Ely Cathedral and took pictures of this lovely edifice.

Introduction to the Commemorative Edition

Included in the scrapbook are pictures of the Ely Cathedral and their automobile. Nan and Peggy toured Lincoln Cathedral, Peterborough Cathedral, the Avon River, and Anne Hathaway's cottage on Stratford-on-Avon, where they spent the night in the Shakespeare Hotel. The pair then journeyed to Paris, enjoying Versailles, the Champs-Élysées, and the Arc de Triomphe. Nan purchased a winter scarf for 190 francs from the "shirtmakers" Rhodes & Brousse on 14 Rue de Castiglione, and then the women had lunch at Fouquet's Restaurant, where they dined on Vouvray, crème, and melon, and they also ordered cigarettes. At Versailles they visited and photographed the Lafayette Memorial.

From Paris they went to Munich and then visited Oberammergau. On July 5, 1934, Nan and Peg left Germany and returned to France, where they visited the Palais des Papes in Avignon, paying a three-franc admission. In Valence they stayed at the Grand Chartreuse. Pictures show the bridge spanning the Rhone River and leading into the city. They paid another three francs to visit the Château de Chaumont. From Valence, Peg and Nan went to Annecy and wound up in Grenoble, documented in the scrapbook with lovely photographs of Château la Caze, built in 1489.

Their Greyelin & Company excursion from Paris, through the Rhone Valley, to Italy, and then to Germany was accomplished in a private motorcar and lasted from June 27 to July 20, 1934. There was a farewell dinner that last night, on a ship of the Red Star Line, the SS *Westernland*, replete with fine cuisine, a concert, and dancing to music performed by the University of West Virginia band.

Dismantling a home that had been in her family since 1805 was a task Nan undertook not only because it had to be done but also

Introduction to the Commemorative Edition

because there was no one else to accomplish it. Part of the poignancy of her task is surely revealed in her description of her joy on returning safely to Belvidere each fall from their sojourn in Eutawville to evade the sickly season:

> As we reached Belvidere, seeing the house waiting there at the head of the wide lawn, serene and lovely, I could feel nothing but a great surge of joy. I wished that I could give the whole place a hug and kiss for opening its gracious arms to us and saying "Welcome Home."[17]

Nan loved horses and rented them for my sister and me at her summer home, High Hills, in Flat Rock, North Carolina. High Hills was an escape from the heat of Charleston and the lowcountry. Built in 1916 by her parents in the Highland Lake Club development, High Hills was Nan's home from May to late August. The house is in the Arts and Crafts style, with wide porches and a screened-in dining porch. All her grandchildren joined her each summer to enjoy the swimming, tennis, horseback riding, and great food.

I used to ride to Flat Rock on the "Carolina Creeper," our name for the Southern Railroad's train from Charleston to the mountains. In those days the cars were still racially segregated. Once aboard I immediately kicked off my shoes and went to sit with my African American friends in the rear car. Nan then met us at the station, and we traveled to High Hills while singing our favorite songs. All the grandchildren slept in one big bedroom. Breakfast was a delight of cornmeal pancakes, scrambled eggs, bacon, and sausages, but before we ate, we had to kneel down and listen to Nan lead morning prayers. I remember well my embarrassment when my first boyfriend

Introduction to the Commemorative Edition

came to visit and realized that he too would have to kneel for the morning-prayer ceremony.

Nan's chief passion in life after horses and grandchildren was gardening. On her grave is this epitaph:

> GRANT ME THIS PRAYER, OH LORD:
> THAT WHEN MY EYELIDS CLOSE
> IN LAST LONG SLEEP,
> I MAY WAKE TO FIND MY HAND UPON A GARDEN GATE,
> TO WANDER DOWN A GARDEN PATH
> BORDERED WITH THOSE DEAR GROWING PLANTS
> I LOVED SO WELL IN LIFE.

She and Doc helped raise me, since I traveled from Charleston to Pinopolis to stay with them every weekend. I gardened with Nan, and I hunted deer with Doc in the Gippy rice fields. Nan had a powerful impact on my life and nurtured my love of gardens, as Nan and Doc were avid gardeners. They had three gardens at their Pinopolis home. Doc had a camellia garden that included varieties such as White Queen, Marie Bracey, Pink Perfection, and Donklery. He successfully crossed every species and took his spectacular blooms to garden shows all over South Carolina. Nan had a rose garden with an arbor of yellow and white Lady Banksia roses and a white Cherokee rose. She had old climbing roses, spring bulbs, a display of lavender and purple irises, a banana shrub tree, and sweet-smelling tea olive trees. The Pond Garden was filled with azaleas of every color from lavender to magenta. Nan and Doc inspired me. Whenever I go into a new garden, whether in France, England, Germany, Switzerland, Italy, or here in the States, I close my eyes and compare these

Introduction to the Commemorative Edition

new, natural wonderlands to my memories of my grandparents' gardens. I hear the wind blowing in Nan's "Harpies," her tall pine trees. I see Doc's beagles and hound dogs treeing a squirrel or pointing a covey of quail in the fields beyond the house.

Doc William Kershaw Fishburne was born in Walterboro on April 18, 1880. He graduated from Porter Military Academy in Charleston and then entered the Medical College of South Carolina. Because he had lost an eye while shoeing a horse, he was unable to serve in World War I. Instead he was named both chairman and the examining physician of the local draft board during World War I and World War II. His chief renown was his career as the public health doctor to Hell Hole Swamp. The year after his death, Nan published *William Kershaw Fishburne: Doctor to Hell Hole Swamp*.[18] He and Nan raised the funds to establish the first hospital in Moncks Corner by sponsoring dance parties on Friday nights and soliciting gifts from wealthy plantation owners. When he began his practice, Doc traveled the county in a horse and carriage driven by a black employee, Peter Heyward.

He became medical director of the Berkeley County Health Department in 1930, which he started with one nurse and one room. As his work grew by leaps and bounds, the department outgrew its cramped facilities and moved into ever-enlarged quarters. During his sixty-two years in Berkeley County, he served on the School Board of Education and the Library Board, as vestryman at Trinity Episcopal Church, and as team doctor for the Berkeley High School Stags football team. I fondly recall sitting next to him on the sidelines of every football game.

Doc Fishburne died February 2, 1968. The local newspaper, Moncks Corner's *Berkeley Democrat*, offered this appraisal of the man at the time of his death.

Introduction to the Commemorative Edition

Warm of manner and compassionate of nature, Dr. W. Kershaw Fishburne turned to the field of public health in a desire to help his fellow men. A native of Walterboro, he had lived for many years in Berkeley County. Seeing the need for a hospital at Moncks Corner, he used his wide acquaintance and powers of persuasion to gather contributions for construction. The hospital is one of many monuments to Dr. Fishburne, who has died at age 87. The most rewarding of those monuments is the large number of friends and admirers who mourn his passing. Among his chief interests was hunting. His packs of hounds and bird dogs were renowned in the Low-country. As a squire of Pinopolis, he was a leader in many good causes. He lived a good life and earned the esteem of his neighbors.[19]

Doc Fishburne and Maude Callen (1898–1990), known as "the Angel in Twilight," were featured in *Life* magazine in 1951 as American representatives of the spirit of the Nobel Peace Prize winner Dr. Albert Schweitzer. Miss Maude was a famed African American midwife who worked with Doc at the Berkeley County clinic and provided tireless care to the desperately poor community of Pineville. Doc and Miss Maude delivered babies, and they cured the sick and infirm. The Medical University of South Carolina awards the Maude E. Callen Nursing Scholarship in her memory. She summed up her values in her statement, "Let me live in a house by the side of the road, and be a friend to man."

I love to tell this story about Doc. He went to deliver the seventh baby in a family that already had six girls. He suddenly felt a shotgun in his back, and the husband said, "Dr. Fishburne, if you deliver another girl in this house, you are a dead man!" Doc replied, "Sir, let's have a drink on that." And when the seventh baby girl arrived, the husband was passed out on the floor. My grandfather was my hero in life. He was loyal and devoted to his friends. When his chief nurse at the Public Health Department, Benny Baskins, was dying of breast cancer, Nan would drive Doc down to Roper Hospital to see her every day.

Doc and Nan had a big dining-room table, and all of us were there every weekend. Catherine Beattie (Cat) did the cooking. In my mind's eye, I see Doc at one end of the table and Nan at the other. In between were Benny Baskins, Uncle Moultrie Ball, Aunt Peach (Anne Fishburne Ball), cousins Dr. Joseph Norman Walsh and Anne Moultrie Ball Helms, and my sisters, Emily Wharton Whaley Whipple and Martha Whaley Adams Cornwell. At the table were our mother and our father, Ben Scott Whaley (1909–1987), who offered toasts to long life and good health. Nan celebrated in the evening by playing Irish songs on her Steinway piano, and Nan's touch was beautiful. The piano had been given to her as a wedding present by "Aunty" Elizabeth Allen Sinkler Coxe. I began playing the piano when I was five years old, and the two of us would practice together. Today I have her piano and her music. Whenever I play, I run through "I'll Take You Home Again, Kathleen." That song epitomizes the grief she must have felt at having to leave her beloved home.

How did Nan ever manage to dismantle Belvidere? It was not easy, but instead a daunting task. Only her courage and her love of life enabled her to get through this. She established Little Belvidere, where she moved the homes of many African Americans still living nearby. She moved the black cemetery at Belvidere to a new cemetery near Spring Hill Baptist Church and erected a memorial dedicated "To the glory of God and in affectionate remembrance of all our people of Belvidere Plantation who are in God's safe keeping, this

Introduction to the Commemorative Edition

cemetery has been given." Nan preserved every letter, diary, photograph, memoir, and guest book important to the history of Belvidere and kept them in her Pinopolis home. Because I was a librarian, she gave many of them to me. In the process of discovering my family history, I made a personal commitment to preserving those memories by editing and publishing those valuable records. They have been the sources for four edited works. This commemorative edition of *Belvidere: A Plantation Memory* serves as my final act of homage to Aunt Em and her beloved Belvidere.

In the last chapter of *A Grand Tour of Gardens,* I tell stories of the gardens at Belvidere gardens. My grandmother Nan cared for the main Belvidere garden until it was inundated in 1942 by the Santee Cooper impoundment that created Lake Marion. Nan and Em had moved from Belvidere, but the memories of the garden and the home of their youth went with them. Soon there were wonderful echoes of Belvidere at Em's Gippy Plantation house and garden outside of Moncks Corner, South Carolina, and Nan's thirteen-acre house and garden in Pinopolis, South Carolina. Gradually she filled her farm with a camellia garden, a rose garden, and a wild swamp garden full of azaleas, bay trees, and bamboo. Nan believed that gardens were an extension of the home, rooms to be enjoyed. She created places for sitting, reading, and listening to her "Harpies," the wind singing in her pine trees. There Nan and my mother, Emily Whaley, would sit together, reading aloud or playing bridge. The wedding receptions for my mother, my sister "Miss Em," and myself were held at Nan's house and garden, with guests spilling into the garden areas and onto the broad lawns.[20]

Recent land-shaping events in China remind me of the effects of the Santee Cooper project in Berkeley and Orangeburg Counties. When complete, the Three Gorges Dam on the Yangtze River

Introduction to the Commemorative Edition

in China flooded river valleys, some under as much as four hundred feet of water, which forced the abandonment of thousands of ancient villages, cities, farms, business, and homesteads. The poignant loss of these structures, lands, and historical and religious sites brought to my mind the flooding of Belvidere in 1942, the year of my birth. The contrast between the lively society of Belvidere as depicted in letters, diaries, photographs, and artworks and the watery bleakness that surrounded me as I stood on the remains of Belvidere's front steps in 2008 was stark. In that year drought shrunk the size of Lake Marion and once again permitted the Belvidere descendants—Sinklers and African American—to visit the site of their forebears' hallowed house and gardens in a testimony to their affection for the place and for each other.

NOTES

1. The South Carolina Public Authority Service, also called Santee Cooper, envisioned providing electrical power, industrial and business development, and modernization to lowcountry South Carolina. Other Santee Cooper goals included controlling floods, reducing disease on the Santee River, and creating a defense industry. For information on Santee Cooper and New Deal South Carolina, see Jack Hayes, *South Carolina in the New Deal* (Columbia: University of South Carolina Press, 2001); David Robertson, *Sly and Able: A Political Biography of James F. Byrnes* (New York: W. W. Norton, 1994); Walter Edgar, *South Carolina: A History* (Columbia: University of South Carolina Press, 1997); Douglas Bostick, *Sunken Plantations: The Santee Cooper Project* (Charleston, S.C.: History Press, 2008); and an unpublished work by Elizabeth Marie Harvey Lovern, "Cultural Models, Landscapes, and Large Dams: An Ethnographic and Environmental History of the Santee Cooper Project, 1938–1942" (dissertation, University of Georgia, 2007). There were many lawsuits brought by people who owned plantations and land. All were settled prior to the impoundments.

Introduction to the Commemorative Edition

2. See *Between North and South: The Letters of Emily Wharton Sinkler, 1842–1865,* edited by Anne Sinkler Whaley LeClercq (Columbia: University of South Carolina Press, 2001), 138–56, for descriptions of life at the Belvidere and Eutaw plantations, steamboat trips on the Cooper River, concerts in Charleston with Jenny Lind, and a jousting tournament at Pineville, South Carolina. At the lancing tournament there were thirty knights with their lances glittering, flags flying, and trumpets sounding. Emily Wharton sat in a ladies stand with two hundred other women from the lowcountry.

3. Charles Sinkler (1818–1894) began cotton farming at Belvidere. He also raised hundreds of acres of short-staple cotton at the Eutaw and Apsley plantations. In the first five decades of his life, cotton culture and slavery were synonymous. By 1860 South Carolina had more than four hundred thousand enslaved African Americans, 52 percent of the state's population, and South Carolina had also exported more than two billion pounds of cotton worldwide. After the Civil War, Charles Sinkler and his family returned to Philadelphia. Charles had hired an overseer to manage Belvidere, but the arrangement was unsuccessful. The family returned to Belvidere and resumed life planting cotton and raising crops. Many former slaves returned to Belvidere and lived on "the street," working for the Sinklers' tenants as day laborers. *Between North and South*, 30, 42, 188–89, 197.

4. Lewis DeSaussure (1865–1934) and Rosena Rivers DeSaussure (1867–1939) were the chief servants at Belvidere during the twentieth century. Their granddaughter Julia DeSaussure Hall (1927–2009) lived at Belvidere as a child. She was thirteen years of age in 1940, when the plantation was dismantled and she witnessed the removal of African American graves from Belvidere to the New Belvidere Cemetery adjacent to Spring Hill Baptist Church.

5. See this volume, page 45.

6. Belvidere guest book, 1901–December 1915, in the possession of Ann Moultrie Helms.

7. See this volume, pages 78–79.

8. Belvidere guest book, 1916–1939, in the possession of Ann Moultrie Helms.

9. The excursion is recounted in *Elizabeth Sinkler Coxe's Tales from the Grand Tour, 1890–1910,* edited by Anne Sinkler Whaley Leclercq (Columbia: University of South Carolina Press, 2007), 95–106.

Introduction to the Commemorative Edition

10. Emily Whaley, *Mrs. Whaley and Her Charleston Garden* (Chapel Hill, N.C.: Algonquin Press, 1997), 90.

11. See this volume, page 72.

12. For a full description of the Pinopolis house, see Emily Whaley, *Mrs. Whaley and Her Charleston Garden*, 111–23.

13. For more information of the life of Charles and Emily Sinkler at Belvidere, read *An Antebellum Plantation Household: Including the South Carolina Low Country Receipts and Remedies of Emily Wharton Sinkler* (Columbia: University of South Carolina Press, 1996) and *Between North and South: The Letters of Emily Wharton Sinkler, 1842–1865* (Columbia: University of South Carolina Press, 2001), both edited by Anne Sinkler Whaley LeClercq.

14. The unpublished love letters of Charles St. George Sinkler to Anne Wickham Porcher Sinkler describe life at Belvidere Plantation and reveal a budding relationship between two young people born in Eutawville but who grew up in quite different communities. These letters are in the possession of Anne Sinkler Whaley LeClercq.

15. See this volume, page 51.

16. See this volume, pages 50–51.

17. See this volume, page 49.

18. Anne Sinkler Fishburne, *William Kershaw Fishburne: Doctor to Hell Hole Swamp* (Columbia, S.C.: R. L. Bryan, 1969).

19. *Berkeley Democrat* of Moncks Corner, S.C., undated clipping, circa February 3, 1968, in possession of Anne Sinkler Whaley LeClercq.

20. Anne Sinkler Whaley LeClercq, *A Grand Tour of Gardens: Traveling in Beauty through Western Europe and the United States* (Columbia: University of South Carolina Press, 2012), 179–78.

Anne Sinkler Fishburne on joggling board

Thomas Isaac Wharton

Frederic S. LeClercq with Carrie Sinkler, Emily Sinkler, and Elizabeth Stevens Martin

Anne Sinkler Fishburne's wedding portrait

Kershaw and Anne Sinkler Fishburne's wedding

Pinopolis House

Benny Baskins and Anne Moultrie Ball Helms at the Pinopolis house

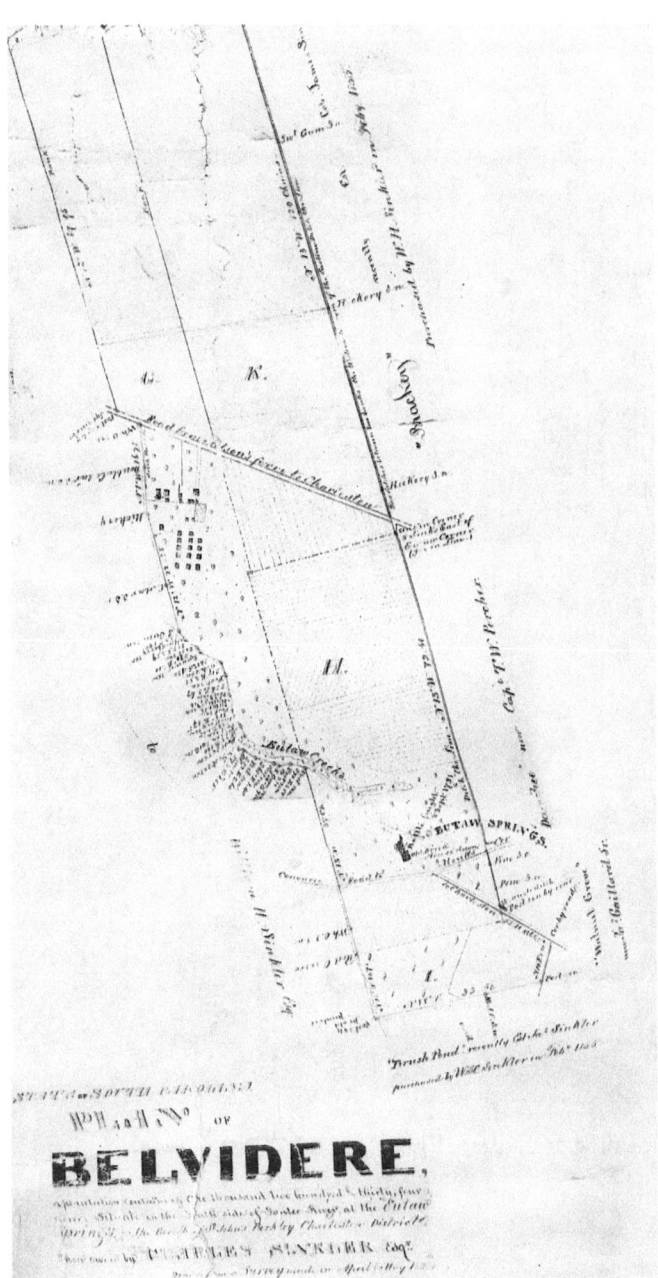

Plat of Belvidere

Garden Walk, Belvidere. Photograph by Stan Lewis

Charles St. George Sinkler.

Anne Wickham Porcher Sinkler
on her wedding day

Wedding party of Emily Sinkler and Nicholas Guy Roosevelt

At the races at Belvidere racetrack

Mule races at Belvidere racetrack

Eutaw Plantation

Caroline Sidney Sinkler

Emily Wharton Sinkler

Carrie and Anne Sinkler at the races

Sinklers on the Belvidere front porch

Lewisfield Plantation, by Emily Fishburne Whaley

Jockeys from St. Johns Jockey Club races at Belvidere racetrack

Anne Sinkler Whaley LeClercq atop the ruins of Belvidere Plantation

❊ I ❊

ORANGEBURG, Sept. 26.—*Special: Belvidere Plantation, famed for its beauty, romance and sporting atmosphere from a hundred years or more ago to the present time, is giving way to modern progress in that it is being taken over for inundation in connection with the extensive Santee-Cooper Hydro-electric Project.*

This well known site of the country home and playground of the Sinklers . . . and scene of horse races in the old style . . . with the romantic background of colonial times and characters, is being transferred to the South Carolina Public Service Authority (Santee-Cooper Project).[1]

On the map of lower South Carolina the Santee Reservoir, known as Lake Marion, shows as a large body of water stretching out long, acquisitive fingers into surrounding territory. From the fisherman's boat it appears as a choppy inland sea, sometimes, when the wind is up, beating in angry waves against the great dam impounding it. But along the ragged edges of the lake the water is placid, flooding the lower ground and leaving higher spots

[1] *News and Courier* (Charleston), Sept. 27, 1940.

uncovered. On one of these spits of shore line stands the lonely remnant of Belvidere, beloved home of many generations of Sinklers and a place noted over a long span of years for its fertile, sunny acres and its gardens, its warm hospitality, good food, gay houseparties, and happy family life.

The foundations of the house, built of mellow, hand-molded brick, overgrown now with wisteria and periwinkle, suggest the height and size of the building. The chance visitor may distinguish still the location of the main rooms, the width of the piazzas. Part of the garden wall remains in a rough tangle of shrubs, vines, and undergrowth. Beyond a quiet stretch of water a portion of the lawn, dotted with the stumps of old oaks and cedars, can still be seen. All the rest of the home site, the adjoining Negro quarters, the race track, lawns, gardens, and fields lie under the waters of the lake, too deep for any eye but that of memory to reach.

Belvidere Plantation was situated on a triangle of land between the clear limestone waters of Eutaw Creek on the south and the swift-running currents of the great Santee on the north. To the west, large brick gateposts topped with white urns marked the entrance to a wooded bluff where the Revolutionary battle of Eutaw Springs was fought and where remants of the British fortifications can still be seen. At the crest of this bluff there were outcroppings of creamy limestone, and the colored people of Belvidere had favorite legends of mermaids sitting on these rocks on moonlight nights combing their long hair with silver combs. At the base of the bluff a bold spring gushed from between the greenish stone ledges and cascaded into the creek, thus getting the name of "the Big Boiler." So crystal clear was this water that, drifting on the surface of the creek in a canoe, one could see enchanting little colored pebbles and conch shells, vivid water plants and the flickering sunshine and shadows on the pinkish sands below. Small water creatures darted in and out of the deep crevasses and caves in the rocks. Overhead hung a canopy of cypress and gray moss, intermingled in spring with the red "keys" of budding maples; along the banks dogwood and pinkbud bloomed in profusion and there were wide beds of wild violets and white swamp lilies.

On the other side of the bluff the ground fell away so sharply that there was only a steep ridge between the Big Boiler and a much smaller spring which was connected with it by a subterranean passage. People used to say that in the time of the early settlers an Indian lad successfully swam through this underground channel; but, urged by some white traders to make a second attempt for the wager of a bottle of whiskey, he never reappeared.

After leaving the bluff, the road wound for a mile through park-like woods of pine, cedar, and holly. It was here, driving home from an Ash Wednesday service at the Rocks Church in 1863, that grandfather Charles Sinkler's horse took fright and bolted, throwing grandmother Emily violently against a tree and killing her instantly. This part of the road was closed thereafter and never used again. A second pair of gates opened onto a 25-acre lawn dotted with great cedars and live oaks and kept smoothly cropped by a flock of sheep. The house, two-storied on a full brick basement, had a piazza with slender round columns across the entire front, and a large wing on one side was balanced by an open, brick-paved sun piazza on the other. It stood on a gentle slope at the crest of the wide lawns, nestled in red oaks, hickory, and cedars, with the gardens to the left and the Negro quarters, or "street," beyond. To the right were more woods and then the long fields of corn and cotton stretching to the river where an occasional freight boat stopped for business at Sinkler's Landing.

There are few very early records of Belvidere to be found but there appears on a Sinkler family tree [2] a note of a grant of 590 acres in Craven County, South Carolina, made by George III to James Sinkler, dated August 14, 1770. This tract was later known as Old Sinkler's or Old Santee. The abounding fertility of this section of the state was described by Samuel DuBose in his *Reminiscences of St. Stephen's Parish* in these terms:

About twenty years before the revolutionary war, the belt of land bordering on the Santee River, through the whole extent of the Parish of St. Stephen's, was the garden spot of South-Carolina. . . . A breadth of three or four miles of swamp as fertile as the slime of the Nile could have made it, was safe for cultivation; and its margins were

[2] An abridged version of the Sinkler genealogical table appears on p. 109.

thickly lined with the residences of as prosperous a people as ever enjoyed the blessings of God. . . . The exceeding fertility of the soil rendered labor scarcely necessary to make it a wilderness of vegetable luxuriance. The great quantity of decomposing matter, and the myriads of insects incident thereto, and the abundant yield of seeds furnished by the rank weeds and grass, caused the poultry yards to teem with a well fed population, and the pastures of crab grass and cane, which are yet proverbial, poured into the dairies streams of the richest milk and enlivened the scene at noon and evening, with the lowing of herds of fat cattle. Nor were swine in abundance, and countless fish of the finest quality from the exhaustless river, wanting to fill up the measure of the people's comforts. Before the eye, was spread, Nature in all her majesty and beauty. . . .[3]

For some years Captain Sinkler, who was the son of a Scotch immigrant, planted Old Santee successfully but recurrent freshets from the river ruined the crops on his low acres in spite of embankments which he and his brother Peter Sinkler [4] of Lifeland Plantation built. After this vain

[3] Samuel DuBose, *Reminiscences of St. Stephen's Parish, Craven County, and Notices of her old Homesteads*, Charleston, 1858, pp. 3-4. This pamphlet is bound in with DuBose's *Address . . . Black Oak Agricultural Society . . .* (see below n. 4) but is given separate pagination.

[4] Peter Sinkler was a Revolutionary patriot betrayed to the British by his brother-in-law, James Boisseau. During absences at Lifeland from Marion's camp, Peter Sinkler would use in emergency a hiding place in the nearby swamp. Boisseau covertly introduced some enemy soldiers to this place of concealment and arranged that others should approach the house by the avenue. Sinkler was thus taken as he sought refuge in the swamp. His property was ransacked and he died of typhus fever shortly afterwards in the southeast room of the Post Office cellar, Charleston. (Samuel DuBose, *Address . . . Black Oak Agricultural Society . . ., April 27, 1858 . . .,* Charleston, 1858. p. 6.)

effort to control the high waters, he and other planters of St. Stephen's Parish decided to shift their crops to safer lands in St. John's Parish. The move took place about 1790 and they there began to experiment with growing cotton. According to contemporary records "in 1799 . . . Capt. James Sinkler, at Belvidere, from a crop of three hundred acres realized the amount of two hundred and sixteen pounds per acre, for much of which he received seventy-five cents per pound. . . ."[5]

It appears that Capt. James Sinkler never moved to Belvidere but that he kept a very efficient overseer there under whose direction the plantation prospered. He died in 1800 and it was between that date and 1803 that his widow Margaret (Cantey) Sinkler had the Belvidere house built and moved there with her family. Her son William Sinkler inherited a great love of horses and horse racing and did much to encourage the development of this sport in South Carolina. When he came to marry, William built on Eutaw Plantation which is separated from Belvidere only by the gently flowing creek, and there laid out a race track where his own racers were trained. Another race track was built at Belvidere over a hundred years later by one of his direct descendants.

DuBose also gives a contemporary estimate of the sequestered property of Peter Sinkler which included such items as twenty thousand pounds of indigo, three thousand bushels of grain, sixteen blooded horses, twenty-eight blooded mares and fillies, one hundred and thirty head of stock cattle, one hundred and fifty head of sheep, two hundred hogs, twenty thousand rails and fifty-five negroes. (Samuel DuBose, *Reminiscences of St. Stephen's Parish*, pp. 9-10.)

[5] Samuel DuBose, *Address . . . Black Oak Agricultural Society . . .*, p. 10.

To Eutaw Plantation there came in 1842 Emily Wharton of Philadelphia, bride of William's son Charles. Letters which she sent back to her father, Thomas Wharton, have been preserved among family papers and bring us graphic pictures of the country life of the ante-bellum period.

Eutaw, December 5th, 1842

Dear Papa,

I was very glad to receive your letter on Thursday. I had been on the lookout for some time and at last at 6 o'clock in the eve I saw the boy come galloping up the avenue with the bag on his arm. It was brought to me and I was delighted to find one in your handwriting as I expected a treat. You ask how I pass my time. Breakfast is from half-past eight to quarter of nine. I get up a little after seven. Mr. Sinkler, five mornings out of seven, gets up at four or five and mounts a horse and goes off to shoot English wild ducks or deer, or to fox hunt. All the family assemble at breakfast at which there is a great variety of hot cakes, waffles, biscuits. Soon after breakfast our little carriage comes to the door and we're off to take a drive. The whole equipage is quite COMME-IL-FAUT. *The carriage is perfectly plain, just holding two persons. The horses are very dark brown with plain black harness. When we set out the dogs come running up so we have a cortege of two greyhounds and two terriers generally. We are always preceded by the groom Samson on horseback to open gates. We are home by twelve or one and then I read, sew etc. until din-*

ner time. Mr. Sinkler goes off with his brothers to hunt and shoot partridges until dinner. They are always, as you see, on horseback. . . . We dine between half-past three and four. Sister Eliza [6] is an excellent housekeeper.

The ice cream and jelly here are the best I ever tasted.

In the evening we have music, both piano and guitar. . . .

Love to all from your affectionate daughter,
Emily

These musical evenings were famous in the neighborhood and frequently the parlor would be filled with friends and neighbors who had come to listen. Emily and her sister-in-law Mrs. William Sinkler both had lovely voices and sang duets.

After the first Christmas in her new southern home, Grandmother Emily wrote her father a delightful description of its charm and novelty.

Eutaw, December 29th, 1842

My dear Papa,

. . . How much amused you would have been at everything here. Early on Christmas morning before crack of day the negroes began to arrive from the different plantations of Mr. Sinkler and I was soon awakened by a loud knocking at my door and then "Merry Christmas Mas' Charlie, may you live many, many year. Merry Christmas Miss Emily, long life and CROSPERITY *to you!" They went*

---

[6] Elizabeth Allen Sinkler, sister of Charles, who married Colonel Richard I. Manning and was mother of South Carolina's Governor R. I. Manning.

to every door in the house and made some such speech. One went to brother James and said "Merry Christmas, Massa, may you live t'ousand year and have to drive you hosses al de time." As soon as I came out of my room I was surrounded by all the house servants eager to "catch" me, that is, to say "Merry Christmas" first. Such laughing and screaming you never heard. Before breakfast every one takes a glass of egg-nog and a slice of cake. It is the universal custom and was not on this occasion omitted by any-one. As Christmas was kept during four days egg-nog was drank regularly every morning. After breakfast a most amusing thing took place. Every four or five minutes companies of women arrived to give their presents and wish Merry Christmas. They bring as presents each about half a dozen eggs and although they were all intended for Missy (Sister Eliza) I insisted upon having half, always to their great delight. I managed to collect about 100 eggs which of course the next day I gave to Eliza for her domestic purposes. All of the negroes had presents of new clothes made to them and it was a perfect babel. Their Massa stood out on the piazza helping them and of course a great deal of attention was paid to me as being "Mas' Charlie new lady." Both he and I were very much congratulated all Christmas morning. . . . Give my best love to Mama and tell her I will write to her next mail day.

    Goodbye, dear Papa,
    Your affectionate daughter, Emily.

Another letter, dated October 7, 1844, sent to Mr. Wharton from Charleston, tells of visiting both there and in Columbia.

Dearest Papa,

We got here safely on Friday the 4th and found everything waiting for us and the city delightfully cool and PERFECTLY *healthy. There has not been a single case of yellow fever or any other fever in Charleston the whole summer. Last week there was not a single white death and only two black. . . . I spent a short time in Columbia most delightfully with Mrs. Manning. The people there are the most hospitable I ever saw and I have made all sorts of promises for visits this winter. People here think no more of asking me to spend the week with them than you would in Philadelphia of inviting them for tea. I have promised to spend the time of the session with Mrs. Hampton. They are all a very generous family and just when I was there gave 15 thousand dollars to build a new Episcopal Church in Columbia.*[7]

Lizzie[8] *and I are very glad to be at the end of our journeyings for some time and we are so pleasantly fixed here—*

---

[7] There is reference to this incident in *Trinity Church, Columbia, S. C., One Hundred and Twenty-Fifth Anniversary 1937*, Columbia, p. 17:

"It is said that the Hampton family alone offered to build this church, but that the wise Rector, Dr. Shand, insisted that the funds be raised by popular subscription. This was done. Probably the Hamptons contributed liberally, but the building was the embodiment of the desires and the work of the congregation as a whole."

Under Dr. Shand's leadership, the cornerstone was laid in 1846 and the building completed at the cost of approximately $12,000.

[8] Lizzie was the first-born of Emily and Charles Sinkler. She later became Mrs. Charles Coxe of Philadelphia and is referred to later as "Aunty."

James and William Sinkler's families and ourselves all living together. Lizzie is enchanted with the children.

Mrs. Middleton sent for me as soon as I got here and has been very kind in invitations. Mr. Sinkler is at the Navy Yard today so he cannot send you any message but he will write to you very soon. He is a great deal there and it is a very disagreeable place. He is the only officer there and the sailors are all negroes who are constantly in mutiny and he has the most unpleasant scenes—indeed I never feel perfectly easy. The Commodore is never there and there is but one white man beside himself at the Yard. . . . He hardly gets home before some one comes running for him to come back over there. . . .

Believe me ever your affectionate
E. S.

The Northern bride soon became greatly interested in the sport of horse racing which was so much featured in this section of the state. One of many letters referring to these local events is that of February 1843.

My dear Papa:

. . . The races are just beginning in a country town about twenty miles from here and the gentlemen are full of it. The races begin tomorrow and last for three days. The Charleston races begin next week. They have sent five horses from the stables here but only one, however, belongs to Eutaw—the rest are sent here to be trained. Jeanette Berkeley is the name of our horse and she is going to run both here and in Charleston and they think she has a

good chance. It is ridiculous the care they take of them. Each horse has two boys to take care of it and a groom to take care of all of them. The horses eat the most dainty food and have to be rubbed with whiskey and actually drink it too. Every day they take exercise they eat twenty eggs! One named Kate Converse used to belong to William [Sinkler] and he sold it to Mr. Sinkler for 3000 dollars after she had made 500 dollars in a race....

The Joust or Tournament was the most colorful feature of the social life of the horse-loving gentry and Grandmother Emily gives a vivid account of one of them in another letter, dated April 25, 1851:

... Wednesday was as bright and beautiful a day as could be desired and as cool as could be desired. Anna and I accompanied by Charles and the Beau-pere, Lizzie, Wharton and Henry,[9] repaired to the ground and took our places in the ladies stand. As we arrived early we got excellent places and had time to inspect the premises before the show began. There were about two hundred ladies present, some in carriages but mostly in the stand and from various parts of the country, from Columbia and Charleston. There were also strangers. The judges' stands were decorated with flags etc. and directly in front of the ladies stand was the Rigg suspended, it must be confessed, from something looking very much like a gallows. At last along the

---

[9] The persons mentioned here were a sister of Charles Sinkler, Anna, and his children, Lizzie and Wharton. "Beaupere" was Emily's name for her father-in-law, Mr. William Sinkler, and Henry was her brother who was evidently visiting her at this time. In this letter she speaks of her husband as "Charles" rather than as Mr. Sinkler as before.

winding road the "Knights" were seen approaching at full speed, the trumphets sounding and as they drew near the band struck up Yankee Doodle—of all things for this anti-yankee state! At last they came before the stage, 30 in all, lances glittering and flags flying and after some maneuvering the steeds were drawn up, lances lowered and the ladies saluted. Mr. Mazyck Porcher [10] *was the King at Arms very handsomely dressed in Sir Walter Raleigh style. He directed the whole affair and deserves great credit. . . . He was attended by a Moor in full costume whose duty it was to pick up the ring when it fell which he did with great solemnity. He was a highly respected old negro belonging to Mr. Porcher and before going off one of the ladies said to him. "Now if you do your part well you will be rewarded," upon which he answered "Thank you, ma'am, all I wish is to have my Moor's dress for my burial suit."*

William Sinkler (Charles' brother) was herald; his dress was very handsome blue velvet trimmed with silver, hat plumes, gauntlets, etc. His horse was beautifully caparisoned. After the saluting was over, the tilting began. The object was to carry off the ring on the lance, a very difficult matter. Each knight came full speed, pointing his lance directly at the ring, many throwing it off on the ground and many failing entirely. At each attempt the trumpet would sound and the Herald and the Master of the Horse would announce the title of the knight. When each of the 27 had had a trial, they defiled past the place of

[10] Mazyck Porcher was the son of Samuel Porcher of Mexico Plantation and the great-great uncle of the author.

starting. There were six trials and when it was all concluded, the Judges pronounced that the Knight of Carolina, a young man by the name of Morton Waring, had carried off the ring the greatest number of times and therefore was directed to choose a Queen which the poor youth did with great trepidation. He chose Miss Elizabeth Porcher. After this the Judges selected the Knight whose costume was the handsomest and he who had ridden most gracefully. Our friend Julius Porcher,[11] *"Knight of Walworth," was chosen for the former and Keating Palmer, "Knight of The Grove," for the latter. Julius Porcher's dress was a full suit of armor which was certainly appropriate and looked extremely well on horseback. He was very ceremonious in his conduct and when requested to select a maid-of-honor did so with much circumstance, pointing his lance and exclaiming in a voice "I'll select the fair Lady Inglesby."*

Then came the ceremony of crowning. The victorious knight crowned the Queen with a wreath of white roses and she in return crowned him with a wreath of laurel. The

[11] Julius Porcher was the son of Thomas and Elinor (née Gaillard) Porcher of Walworth Plantation. A pamphlet by Frederick A. Porcher, *Upper Beat of St. Johns, Berkeley*, 1868, has this reference to his death in the Confederate War:

"In the army he rose to the rank of Lieut. Col. . . . With that rank he entered the fatal field of Chickamauga, or Missionary Ridge (Sept. 19th & 20th, 1863) & was never more seen by his friends. No effort could ever recover his body. On that fatal day perished this young man, the joy & hope of his family, the pride & honor of his name, the hope & ornament of his country."

Walworth was purchased some time before 1828 by Major Samuel Porcher for his son Thomas. It was named after a village near London where Samuel Porcher was educated.

other two knights then, kneeling, received from the hands of their maids-of-honor the one a scarf for the best costume and the other a pair of spurs for the best riding. This over, the Herald (William) in the name of the King at Arms, the Master of the Horse and himself, invited the knights and the company to a collation to which of course all repaired. It was by this time three o'clock and the collation being very much like a supper at a ball, was very acceptable. In the evening there was a regular ball given by the knights to which Charles, Anna and I did not go. . . . The whole affair, to sum up, was very handsome and went off with but one interruption which nearly broke Lizzie's heart. A young man, Rene Ravenel, the Knight of Berkeley, rode a vicious horse much against his father's wish and on the first trial as he approached the Ring he lost all command of the animal and in a few moments was thrown. Fortunately, he was only marred, not hurt and in a few moments mounted another horse, came before the ladies stand accompanied by the Herald and the Master of the Horse and after lowering his lance said "The Knight of Berkeley comes before you without plume or spurs and craves the indulgence of the ladies for his disgrace." He is quite a handsome young man and looked extremely pale and disconcerted. It was too much for poor Lizzie who burst into tears and thought of no one else all day. He went immediately to his father's carriage and Lizzie was somewhat relieved by the ladies sending him a bunch of flowers with a very complimentary message, requesting him to favor them with his company at the stand which he accordingly did and was quite as much a hero as the real victor—women, you know, having always a penchant for the knights in misfortune. The rest of the riders acquitted themselves to admiration—in this part of the world they seem to be one with the horse and there were some splendid horses there. They were, of course, picked horses and I heard Mr. Brevort of N. Y. who was present saying that after seeing such splendid riding and horses, he could never mount a horse again. Our friend FitzSimons came very near getting the greatest number of rings. He was the Knight of Erin, dressed in green velvet with gold shamrocks on his hat, which was a French affair with plumes, and on his coat a scarf on which was embroidered the harp etc. of Ireland. There were many other handsome creatures, particularly Saladin, the Knight Templar, the Hungarian Knight and the Knight of Malta.

Now I am afraid I have tired you with this long account. I had no idea of going so much into detail when I began but my pen ran almost without my knowing it....

Later letters from Emily Sinkler were written from Belvidere where she and her family were then settled. In February 1852 she tells her brother Henry of her first months there.

... It seems strange to hear of snows in the letters I receive. We have had here for more than a fortnight the most delightful spring-like weather, weather in which one feels comfortable both out of doors and in. I am taking advantage of it to improve the place.... Charles has given

me a carpenter to work under my direction for a month and a person to garden, so my hands are full. The old garden is to be restored—it is now nearly forty years since it was tended but it contains many shrubs yet. I have arranged a small garden on each side of the front steps which is to be enclosed with an iron fence and is to contain the choicest specimens. I have already some very fine roses which have taken so well that they will bloom this spring. The Glory of France, Groille, Harrisonian de Brunnius, Cloth of Gold and Souvenir de Malmaison. This last is the most splendid rose you ever saw—as large as a coffee cup and so firm and rich. I am foraging all through the country for roots and cuttings....

Another letter to her father at about the same time is of interest because of its reference to mail and parcel deliveries.

My dear Papa:

The box arrived on Sunday afternoon in good order though it had not been without its adventures. It came from Charleston up to the 31 mile station on Saturday and that night the store it was lodged in took fire and was burned to the ground. They saved the box, though a vehicle of Charles which was sent for it got injured and they had some difficulty in saving the mule from the stable. You can imagine the excitement the opening of the box caused and the screams of delight which hailed the debut of each fresh object. The note paper is perfect and just the thing I wanted for I used the last sheet of my old note paper today.

You cannot doubt but that the stamped envelopes were very acceptable. These stamped envelopes appear to be universally used now—in all my numerous correspondence I have received but two letters unstamped since July. An old lady of our acquaintance carries her use of them rather far, for she puts them on letters she sends by private opportunities.

We intended going to Charleston next week but I feel rather doubtful about it. . . . I would be sorry to have to give up the trip for the beau-pere has engaged rooms for us at the Charleston Hotel. I couldn't go at a better time for the beau-pere will have his carriage and horses and servants there. . . .

The Philadelphia Whartons frequently came to visit at Belvidere and all of them seem to have fallen in love with it. On one such visit, Emily's sister Mary, writing home to her brother Henry, gives us a visitor's commentary:

. . . Mr. Sinkler has gone up for a few days to his new place and as the Mannings all went too, it is quite deserted here. We went to a regular country wedding on Thursday which was rather amusing. . . . The dancing was of a most violent description, but they did not get to a reel before I left, the which I should have liked to see. Your friend Miss Patsie was there in quite full dress—viz bare arms and neck and a muslin dress and white satin sash. I think you have made quite an impression on her as she often spoke of you.

We had a beautiful dinner at old Mr. Sinkler's last Tuesday. You would scarcely suppose yourself in the country from the variety and elegance of the entertainment.

There is a very good piano at the Eutaw and I go over to play almost every afternoon and my performances have been very much admired. Emily and Anna sing beautifully together. It is really wonderful to hear such grand music in the country. . . .

The five children of Charles and Emily—Lizzie, Wharton, Mary, Caroline and Charles St. George—grew up at Belvidere, Charles succeeding his father as master there. His wife was Anne Wickham Porcher, daughter of Col. Julius Porcher of St. Julien's Plantation (mentioned heretofore as Knight of Walworth at the jousting match) and Belvidere prospered under their love and care.

❊ II ❊

THE sound of winter rain drip, dripping on the roof takes me back as if by magic to other nights of long ago when, as a child cosy and warm under the covers, I would wake to hear the other cold rains beating against the nursery windows and gurgling through the gutters of Belvidere, and the rise and fall of the wind through the bare branches of the red oaks around the house. In a lull I would hear from Maum Hetty's hill in the Negro quarters the far-off honking of her geese, adding eeriness and mystery to the dark night and deepening my own sense of security and warmth as I snuggled farther under the covers.

I remember at Maum Hetty's house a dim room lit only by a bed of glowing coals, the old lady sitting by her wide fireplace in a hand-made arm chair worn slick with long use and at her feet on the hearth a big iron pot. Smaller ones simmered on the coals and the contents of these pots were a never-ending source of interest to us as we were always given a liberal taste of whatever they held. Sometimes it would be collard greens that had been cooking with a big piece of fat bacon and a red pepper since early morning. Occasionally it would be stew of " 'gator" or of some other creature from the swamps. Whatever it was, to our childish taste nothing ever tasted quite so good as the food that Maum Hetty cooked.

Often we children would draw up on three-legged stools and listen with rapt absorption to Maum Hetty's tales of the Guinea Negroes of whom her father was one before he was brought as a slave to Carolina. Sometimes she taught us scraps of native African songs, and when we were able to count to ten in African we concluded that our education was complete indeed. Sometimes she would tell stories about Daddy Duck Peter, her husband. He was Grandpa Charles Sinkler's foreman, and when spring cotton chopping time came around and more hands were needed, he would stand on the hill in "the street" and call, and presently along the paths leading from the nearby plantations would come colored people of all sizes with hoes over their shoulders, glad for a day's work.

In recollection I can also hear through the still evening air of spring the sound of Daddy Major's bugle, letting not only the Belvidere negroes but those of adjoining plantations know that there would be prayer meeting that night. Later, after supper, might come the treat of being allowed to go up to the little church in the quarters, slip into a dark back seat and hear Daddy Major read a "potion" from the Bible by the flickering light of a chimneyless kerosene lamp, pronouncing the words most fearsomely and strangely. He would then launch forth into his sermon, warning his congregation that at some time to all of us death would come riding on a pale horse and "hitch him at de do'." Then would we "study 'bout prayin' " but for many it would be too late. To the faithful, he promised a certain reunion in the sweet bye and bye, "skipping on a sea of glass." Then would come the spirituals and "shouting" which before the evening was over would have the whole congregation rocking in a frenzy of song and throbbing rhythm. I have often seen a sleeping baby passed from person to person as the urge to get up and "shout" would seize the holder, until at last it would end up, still sleeping, in the skimpy little lap of a child not much bigger than itself.

Another memory is of a warm spring day when, to the tune of creaking harness and wheels crunching in the sand, we drove along the Nelson's Ferry Road to dine at Bloomfield with Cousins Augusta and Augustus Fludd. This brother and sister were a perennial source of interest to us because we had heard that they had been dashingly good looking when young and had never married because each had had a very romantic and unhappy love affair in their younger days. They had both been fine riders and there was a story that Cousin Augusta had once crossed the Santee River on horseback—a spectacular feat as the stream is deep and wide and its currents swift and strong. The Fludd's pew in church was across from ours, and when Mr. Motte would read from the Psalms "Let the floods clap their hands," we would gaze at them surreptitiously, wondering excitedly if they would this time take advantage of this unprecedented indulgence and favoritism on the part of our austere minister!

Dining at Bloomfield included the delights of rich macaroni pies, plum cordial, big bowls of clabber with thick yellow cream on top sprinkled over with brown sugar and nutmeg, and sweet potato pone wonderfully sticky and gooey around the edges. The back piazza at Bloomfield led into the garden which was on a bluff overlooking the Santee with the big swamp beyond. On a shady shelf of the piazza there was always kept a drinking gourd and a cedar bucket of river water which had been drawn early in the morning and left to settle and, though it might be still a bit on the muddy side, no one could persuade us children that this was not the sweetest water in the whole wide world.

One of the most familiar figures on the Belvidere scene was that of Maum Ellen, plump and comely, dressed in neat gingham with crisply starched white apron and head handkerchief. I can see her now sweeping along the path which led from "the street" to the dairy with her cedar "piggin" under her arm. The dairy was near the big house and was a quaint little one-room building with plastered white-washed interior walls with wide pine shelves kept scrubbed white by Maum Ellen. There were no windows but a funny square vent in the steeply sloping roof. Every morning and evening Daddy Lewis brought the pails of milk from the stable yard to the dairy and turned them over to Maum Ellen, who enjoyed to the utmost her prestige as head of the dairy. She was quite a martinet and rarely allowed any of the children, white or colored, to cross the sacred threshold. Occasionally, however, she might let us come into the dim, cool little room and watch her skim the thick yellow cream from the milk which filled long lines of shallow crockery bowls. This cream was collected in a deep crock until it was "ripe." Then she would pour it into a large earthen churn where a half-hour's rhythmic working of the wooden dasher produced, as if by magic, big blobs of golden butter.

Once in a while Maum Ellen would step over to the kitchen house which was nearby to have a little chat with Maum Rebecca, thus leaving the dairy door open and unguarded. Then we might slip in unnoticed and take some of the thick clotted cream to eat with our baked sweet potatoes. But woe betide us if we were so unlucky as to get caught at it!

Along with the dairy and the kitchen, there were clustered at the back of the Belvidere house like small chickens around a mother hen, the wash-kitchen, Maum Rosena and Daddy Lewis' house, and the smokehouse from whose shingled hip roof in pig killing season there filtered thin wisps of blue hickory smoke, evidence that Daddy Major was smoking the hams. Beyond these buildings came the stables and barns, the poultry yards and rye patches for the dairy cows. There was always a busy stir of activity in this back yard world, little colored children running from place to place on errands or passing through to the fields beyond with tin buckets of breakfast or dinner for the cotton choppers and plowmen. Recalling those long-ago days, it is as though there passed before me a procession of dear and familiar friends who so faithfully served our family over many years—Daddy Tom, the dignified butler with his red waistcoat and brass buttons; Satira, the maid, with her pretty smile and ready laughter; Mammy, a devoted nurse; Maum Rebecca, the cook whose hot breads were famous all over the county; Maum Ellen, Daddy Major, Maum Rosena, Daddy Lewis, and many others who now, like Belvidere, are gone except in the memories of those who loved them.

One of our greatest pleasures in a Belvidere childhood was a visit to our Stevens relatives at Northampton. We always had a wonderful time with Greaty and Uncle and each occasion seemed better than the ones before.[12] With Liz and Laura [13] and our little colored playmates we rambled over the plantation and found many excitements in the woods and swamps. We especially liked to go "cokey" hunting with Judy and Tunka who were Laura's and Liz's colored shadows. Judy was big, fat and jolly, very black,

[12] "Greaty and Uncle" were Mr. and Mrs. Charles Stevens. "Greaty" or "Aunt Mames," the daughter of Charles and Emily Sinkler, married "Uncle," the son of Henry Le Noble Stevens and Henrietta (née Gaillard) Stevens. Northampton Plantation became the Stevens home in 1853. Built in 1715, it was once the home of General William Moultrie. Later the noted botanist Henry William Ravenel resided there for some years.

[13] "Liz" or Elizabeth Allen Stevens became Mrs. Alexander Martin of Charleston, S. C.; Laura Stevens, sometimes called "Baby," Mrs. Wyndham M. Manning of Columbia, S. C.

a little older and much larger than the rest of us. Tunka was skinny with bright eyes like a 'possum's. Right after breakfast, which we ate in the pantry with Daddy Quakoo threatening all kinds of bad luck if we left any of our hominy or milk, we would dash off to the swamp which made a horseshoe around the yard. Soon we were picking our way cautiously along a narrow path which led to the center of the swamp, going single file and watching warily for snakes—one morning we counted seventeen. There were many harmless ones such as grass and ribbon snakes, but also poisonous moccasins and rattlers. When we came to a particularly bad stretch of black, slimy mud, Judy "backied" us across. About a half hour's walk would bring us to the creek. Its banks were covered with wild oxalis, bluebells and yellow mustard, and along its shallow edges we would search for cokeys, a small black shellfish something like a clam. We would shriek with delight when we found clusters of them. Laura generally fell in and we would have to pull her out and dry her off the best we could before going back to the house.

We sometimes went for long drives with Uncle to Hanover [14] and Brunswick plantations which he also planted. The roads lay between big fields of cotton and corn and

[14] The house at Hanover Plantation was built in 1716 by Paul de St. Julien, grandson of a Huguenot emigrant, Pierre de Julien de Malacre. Paul married Mary Amy Ravenel, daughter of the emigrant René Ravenel. It was constructed of cypress and was a prize example of the early architectural style. Its chimney was ornamented with the device "Peu a Peu," part of the old French saying "Peu a peu l'oiseau fait son nid." At the time of the Santee Cooper flooding of this area, the house was removed to Clemson, S. C., where it was restored in every detail.

through beautiful woods carpeted with wild flowers of every description. On these drives Uncle, Greaty, and Mother usually sat on the front seat of the open six-seated carriage while on the back seat were as many children as could be crammed in. Greaty loved poetry and often enlivened the drives by repeating verses which we made a game of "capping."

Uncle was a wonderful horseman and loved young, dashing horses. At the time of this particular visit to Northampton he had just bought a pair of very gay ones which Greaty promptly named Hurry and Natty. One afternoon Uncle invited any of us who were not afraid of risking our necks behind them to drive with him to the other plantations. To a man, we were all waiting at the foot of the steps when the carriage and the lunging pair of horses pulled up for a minute. Mother and Greaty managed to jump aboard but to our dismay, off went the carriage, Uncle calling back that he would make a turn round the house and pick up the stragglers on the next stop. We gathered that this was no time to falter so as the carriage reappeared and slowed for a minute alongside us we threw ourselves at it, clutching hold of whatever we could and scrambling on in the nick of time as we headed wildly for the open gate. We sat frozen for a great portion of that ride, not thinking of capping verses or counting the flowers we were spinning past.

Another of Uncle's horses that we all loved, one which was his special saddle horse, was a gorgeous sorrel named

Mark Hanna. When we went fox hunting Mark generally led the field, head up and reddish gold coat shining in the early morning sun, Uncle sitting him straight as an arrow and riding like a Jehu.

I remember one morning when we were all about to start off for a ride, Uncle suddenly looked at Henry [15] sitting on his shaggy little pony and said "Man, you are big enough to ride a real horse now. Get off that pony and get on Mark." Henry was pretty small and Mark looked enormously large. Henry shook his head, but Uncle reached over and pulled him from Pigmy, threw him up on Mark and handed him the reins. He called for another horse for himself and soon we were all galloping along. Mark seemed to understand the situation and behaved like the gentleman he was, though only a few days previously, when Allen Jervey was showing off on him before the girls, he had bolted for the stable door which was slightly open and, to our amusement, had scraped Allen off.

An always delightful event was an invitation to the Northampton household to dine at Woodlawn with Cousin Ellen and Cousin William Ravenel. The grownups went ahead in the open carriage and the children came behind in the two-wheeled plantation cart driven by "Cou' Joshway." Planks had been put across the cart with buggy-blankets folded to make the seats a little softer. On these we perched, looking, I imagine, like rows of young birds,

---

[15] Henry Le Noble Stevens was the only son of "Uncle" and "Greaty" (Mr. and Mrs. Charles Stevens). He was later killed in World War I at the Battle of St. Mihiel in September, 1918.

Belvidere: A Plantation Memory

holding on for dear life as the cart bumped over the rough corduroy roads.

We passed deserted Chelsea [16] with the remains of its house standing in the overgrown garden. One could still see the outlines of the terraces leading down to the lake with its tiny little island where there used to be a rustic garden house. The heavy front door of the house creaked back and forth in the spring breeze and if one looked closely scars of a British cavalry sword could still be seen upon it. Not far away on the road between Biggin and Black Oak Churches [17] was Major Majoribank's tomb on a little rise outside the Wantoot Plantation gate. Daniel Ravenel had had this erected for a young British officer who was wounded at the battle of Eutaw Springs and died at Wantoot on the retreat of the British army.

The Woodlawn house was like what I always imagined a "mansion" to be. It had seventeen rooms and a broad piazza, the long overhanging roof supported by tall, slender pillars which came down to the ground outside the piazza. On top of the house a little roof balcony gave a wide view over the plantation. Cousin Annie told us that from this roof the Woodlawn family had watched the Union troops marching along the Canal Road during one

[16] Chelsea was settled well before the Revolution by Daniel Ravenel, grandson of the emigrant René Ravenel. Pooshee, the colonial home of René Ravenel, was located near the site of Black Oak Church.

[17] Biggin was the parish church of St. John's Berkeley, built about 1712. Black Oak Church was near the old Canal lock. It was removed to Pinopolis and re-erected as a parish house for Trinity Church before the flooding of the area in 1941.

of the raids of the Confederate War. After a delicious dinner eaten in the wide, cool hall, we children would ramble happily over the plantation until time to drive home.

Early in 1904, the Stevens family left Northampton to move to Lewisfield [18] on the Cooper River. Those of us who had loved Northampton and shared its hospitality felt keenly about this change. A dear friend and cousin [19] expressed our sentiment for Northampton in particular and plantation life in general in a letter dated January, 1904, and sent from Winthrop College.

. . . This is the day the Stevens are leaving Northampton forever! I am so sad over it that I feel as though I must talk with some one who feels about it as I do. I know you are thinking, as I am, of the many happy days we have spent at Northampton. I can see the snug, warm parlor in the winter evenings, with all of us playing games or reading, or around the piano lustily singing "Camp Town Race Track" as Cousin Mary rattled off the accompaniment. I am in one of the bright upstairs bedrooms looking out across the green yard, or down into the deep shadows of the dam road; I think of long walks through the woods and

---

[18] Lewisfield Plantation is situated on the west bank of the Cooper River between Gippy and Exeter Plantations. This thousand acre tract was originally known as "Little Landing" and was "transferred" to Sedgwick Lewis by Sir John Colleton, Fourth Baronet, on Sept. 15, 1767, after which this plantation was and still is known as "Lewisfield."

[19] Caroline Palmer Cain (Cazzie), daughter of Dr. Joseph Cain and Mary MacBeth Cain of Somerset Plantation.

the delight of finding the different flowers in their seasons. Do you remember our coming in a far-off spot upon a clump of violets so perfect and lovely that we were touched into silence and then with one accord softly chanted "Full many a flower is born to blush unseen. . . ." But no more of this or I'll begin to cry!

Have you ever been to Lewisfield? I went through the yard once on the way to picnic at Mulberry. It has a fine big house facing Cooper River—"handsome house to lodge a friend, a river at the garden's end." It is really very interesting looking and I have no doubt will be a delightful place to live. I know that in a way Cousin Charlie is very happy over this move for he has always wanted to plant rice and he will now have a chance to expand. Henry is just a little boy who is excited over the change and he will enjoy the river. But to Cousin Mary and Elizabeth and Laura it is a great wrench. So often has Cousin Mary told me of coming to Northampton as a bride, driving through the woods sweet with jessamine and wild plum.

I hope I have not made you any sadder by writing in this way but it has been a relief to me because I know that you understand. The girls up here are very nice but they don't know about plantations and the way we feel about them. A plantation is almost like a person, isn't it? To leave it is like losing someone very dear.

And Greaty wrote to Mother of the throes of moving and resettling.

Belvidere: A Plantation Memory

My dearest Anne: *Lewisfield—Thursday*

We have got here! I am sitting in the parlour, a really beautiful room, as large as the Belvidere one. It is a scene of terrible confusion but the dining room is as home-like as possible, and all fixed by Tom and Quaccoo. We have sent since Saturday, 21 loads of our things, and got off yesterday at 11—the yellow carriage loaded to the top with every variety of thing from a picture of the celebrated Venus to a howling cat in a bag. . . . A feat, leaving the dear old house as bare as your hand, every corner of it, except every picture, the piano and two mirrors. Hennie and St. Clair most kindly stayed to pack and send all of these—most kindly—a tremendous job. . . . I shall never forget the kindness of people. All along the road people met us with good wishes and hot biscuit and coffee. Wagons and mules were lent us all day and every day. Porcher Stoney and John Porcher both met us and welcomed us . . . with beams of welcome and most efficient help in the way of putting up beds, washing of china, making fires; and John with stalwart negroes and wagons for two days. . . . I will not describe the house. Your room and Carry's crib is ready. . . . When you feel like it come. Any day or hour, and any company you have. . . . Now do come for a fortnight, not a day less.

Mary

Needless to say, the 35 miles between Belvidere and Lewisfield was often traveled by both Sinklers and Stevens in the years which followed.

❋ III ❋

BEFORE the time of automobiles and improved roads, a country home like Belvidere was rather isolated. This meant that visitors were always welcome and that instead of spending a few days they would stay for weeks on end. The pleasure given by these visits to both guests and hosts was reflected in numbers of letters saved in the Belvidere cedar chest.

. . . Belvidere is always a place in my memory, and I think in everyone else's who has ever had the happiness of going there, of the most beautifully happy home life, of doing so much for others and of sweet content and beauty. I always feel as if the sun was shining over Belvidere and all of you . . .

. . . Belvidere is the sweetest spot I think I have ever seen anywhere.

. . . I have thought of you and of Belvidere so much on this lovely spring day—how I would love to walk with you through the dear old garden and have you show me the progress of your flowers and vegetables and talk over all that has happened since I was with you. What sweeter

or more congenial spot for family gossip than the dear old Belvidere garden. Don't you wonder sometimes over the many conversations that have taken place there since it first became a garden? . . .

Aunt Kate (Mrs. Henry Wharton of Philadelphia) wrote in her diary at the time of a visit in March 1900:

. . . I find the dear old place lovely as ever and the welcome warms my heart. Anne[20] *has the power of spreading about her an atmosphere of peace and content. We have had several pleasant evenings of music. It is warm as summer, the woods beautiful with yellow jessamine, dogwood, plum and pinkbud.*

Friends would come to stay at irregular intervals, but certain members of the family made an annual event of their return to Belvidere. The advent of Papa's brother, Uncle Wharton, was a source of excitement to the entire plantation. Uncle Wharton was quite a personage in the family. Papa liked to tease him sometimes by calling him "The Great I Am." He deserved our admiration, however, for he went to Philadelphia as a very young man just after the Confederate War in which he served and, after studying under Dr. Weir Mitchell, became one of the most successful doctors in that city. When we visited Lifeland, his summer home in the country near Philadelphia (he named it for Peter Sinkler's plantation on the Santee River), he seemed submerged in the stress and strain of

[20] Mrs. Charles St. George Sinkler (née Anne Porcher), the author's mother.

his big practice and consequently rather stiff and stern. But when he came to Belvidere with some of his cronies for his fall hunting holiday he left his cares behind him and was one of the most delightful and genial people imaginable. Mother and Papa delighted to please him and his friends, and everybody and everything on the plantation was at his disposal.

Luckily for us, the frosts came earlier than usual in the fall of 1902, for Uncle Wharton had written that he wanted to come down to Belvidere with Uncle Arthur, Mr. Coleman, and Dr. Cheston on November 7. Of course this meant that we had to get moved speedily from our summer home in the Pinelands [21] and have everything at Belvidere ship-shape for his arrival. His friends were as determined to enjoy themselves as he was and all were great outdoors-men. Mr. Coleman, of Lebanon, Pa., who raised, trained, and hunted his own dogs, brought down six or eight beauties, so they were well supplied in that

[21] The founding of the villages in the Pinelands dated from 1793 and is described in these words by Samuel DuBose in his *Reminiscences of St. Stephen's Parish* . . ., pp. 31-32.

"After the year 1790, when freshets in the river became more frequent, the climate became more sickly. The residents along the swamp suffered severely from agues and fever, and it was observed with surprise, and it still remains a mystery, that overseers and negroes, and others who lived entirely in the swamp, enjoyed more health than those that lived on the uplands. Capt. James Sinkler, who was a sagacious observer, was led from his observations to believe that a pine land residence, even but a short distance from the swamp, would secure its occupants from fever. Acting on this notion, he built a house for himself in the pine land, and in June 1793, retreated to it with a family, blacks and whites included, of more than twenty persons. In November he returned to his plantation, having passed the summer in the enjoyment of uninterrupted health. This experiment was immediately imitated. Pineville was settled in 1794. . . ."

line. Every morning, after a large old-fashioned breakfast of sausages, hominy, hogshead cheese, hot cakes and batter bread which was eaten very leisurely while the horses and mules were being saddled and the lunch packed, the hunters at last got off in a cavalcade of barking dogs and little colored boys who ran ahead to open the gates. Papa always planned the hunts and went along, and as all our neighborhood was proud and fond of Uncle Wharton, he got many invitations to hunt on other plantations as well. Mr. Coleman and Papa were fine shots and the day's bag usually fell to them, but Uncle Wharton did not seem to mind as what he wanted most was just to get out of doors in the fresh air and sunshine in the familiar countryside.

Before the time of the evening home-coming, Daddy Tom and Satira would make big fires in the parlor, library, and all the bedrooms so that when the hunters arrived, tired and cold, the roaring logs greeted them. They soon got out of boots and hunting clothes and were ready for dinner. On these occasions, Dinah outdid herself, taking special pride in upholding her reputation as a wonderful cook and Mother's as a successful housekeeper. After dinner the men sat around the big fire in the dining room and went over every event of the day—why this dog behaved as he did when they found such and such a covey—why in heaven's name Dr. Cheston couldn't get his gun up in time for the easy shot at that single which just seemed to dare him to shoot. How frustrated cautious Uncle Wharton looked when, standing in the middle of a big covey and taking careful aim all around, he found that his safety was on! How Mr. Coleman should have given such and such a dog a good whipping for flushing and how another dog should have had his lips squeezed for "mouthing" his birds when retrieving. And what a time they all had had getting Uncle Arthur, who looked like the pictures of Santa Claus, off and on his mule! After an hour of this, Uncle Wharton always joined Mother in the parlor and they played backgammon steadily, allowing no one to interrupt them, till bed time.

Sometimes on these holidays, Uncle Wharton and his friends used to make a pilgrimage down to shoot at Cassada, a place famous for its birds. They would drive down in the carriage the evening before with blankets and other paraphernalia, followed by a wagon with their dogs and saddles, and spend the night, sleeping on the fodder and shucks in Daddy Pompey's barn. Mother always sent some cooked provisions with them such as baked ham and biscuits, and Maum Felicia fixed their coffee at Cassada. They enjoyed these jaunts but were invariably glad to get back to Belvidere's good beds, hot fires, and bountiful meals.

On one rainy day, Papa persuaded the huntsmen to stay indoors till after lunch so they all gathered before the dining room fire to clean their guns and oil their boots. Suddenly there came a terrifying explosion followed by a moment's hush and then by a hubbub of voices and the clatter of feet flying from all over the house towards the dining room. There we found Uncle Wharton sitting with his gun in his hands looking rather pale for him and with a very sheepish expression on his face. Around him the others were laughing in a very relieved way and teasing him about what had happened. It seemed that Uncle Wharton, who was one of the most careful and meticulous people in the world—and let us all know it—had neglected to unload his gun when he came in the evening before. As he cleaned it both barrels had gone off, tearing a large, ragged hole in one of the panels of the door. Most fortunately, no one was shot. Uncle Wharton tried his best to make Papa take a five-dollar bill to have the door fixed but Papa laughingly but firmly refused. The door should remain as it was, he said, just to prove that Uncle Wharton was human like the rest of us!

Another yearly event, anticipated eagerly, was the arrival of Aunty and Aunt Cad,[22] who always came down from Philadelphia in April to spend several weeks at Belvidere. During our childhood on the plantation our lives were full of simple and natural delights but thin as to touches with the outside world of cities and city dwellers, and I shall never forget the special excitement of watching the carriage drive up to where we all—Mother, Papa, Em, Cad, and I, the house servants, and a crowd of little colored children—would be waiting to greet these visitors. They would step out in their smart town clothes and,

---

[22] "Aunty" was Mrs. Charles Coxe of Philadelphia, daughter of Charles and Emily Sinkler of Belvidere. Her sister, "Aunt Cad," was Caroline Sidney Sinkler, also of Philadelphia.

throwing their arms around us each in turn, would give us warm, fragrant hugs. To this very day, when I get a whiff of *lait d'iris* or a certain violet perfume, these memories rush over me with a tug of homesickness. Then the thrill and glamour later of seeing their pretty, dainty things unpacked; and among them there was always, to our intense joy, an Easter dress and hat for each of us. There was one particular hat that remains in my memory as the loveliest hat I ever saw. It was a big-brimmed rough white straw with a wreath of white snowballs and green leaves around the crown, and it caused a minor tragedy in my life when it was ruined during a spring downpour which caught us in the open carriage while we were driving over to Walworth for dinner.

When Aunty and Aunt Cad were expected, there was always a mad whirl of preparations. The house was polished and shined from basement to attic and Daddy Tom in his red waistcoat with brass buttons, an apron tied on conspicuously, had a wonderful time bustling about, bossing everybody and doing very little work himself. Mammy always grumbled when Daddy Tom called on her for extra jobs, but secretly she liked it and he managed to get a lot of extra work from her.

Finally, on the morning of the honored guests' arrival, Satira and I fixed for all the rooms big jars of peach and wild plum blossoms and bowls of snowdrops and violets so that the whole house smelt and looked like spring. There were always many callers, both white and colored, when

Aunty and Aunt Cad were with us, and it seemed to me that there was a never-ending stream of Negroes coming up the side steps bringing presents of some kind. The gift might be a squawking chicken or a guinea, or a little bowl of "beat pindar"; more often it was a half-dozen eggs tied up in a questionable looking "hankcher." Aunt Cad, particularly, always listened with affectionate sympathy and interest to the long tales of births and deaths, weddings and woes that had happened since her last visit. And she always sent each caller away beaming, with a new apron or scarf and a piece of money pressed into the hand, receiving in return a hearty "Gawd bless you, Miss Carrie." Nearly every morning some of the little barefoot colored children from "the street" came to the house with bunches of wild violets and Easter lilies for Aunty who loved them, bouquets which were held so tightly in eager little black hands that the stems were warmed and the blossoms drooping.

One year Mother paid a very pretty compliment to Aunt Cad. She estimated the value of the presents of food which the colored people had brought for her and bought as a lasting memento a graceful silver goblet on which was engraved: "Caroline Sidney Sinkler from her people at Belvidere whose hearts she holds as they hold hers."

On Easter Sunday afternoon we had, traditionally, a big gathering at the church in "the street." Aunt Becky Coxe always sent many boxes of Easter eggs for these events —pink, pale green, lilac, and chocolate, so elaborately decorated with curlycues and fancy lettering of white icing that the eyes of the colored people would almost pop out of their heads with delight. Mother would have a short service first, then Aunt Cad would give a talk followed by a few words from Aunty and then the singing would start, such singing that the church fairly rocked with it. After this we would give out the Easter eggs, a ceremony which lasted until sundown as there were always several hundred in the congregation.

Aunt Cad returned to Belvidere yearly as long as it was there to come to. Before she came down in the spring of 1932 she wrote that she would like to go again to Milford [23] where she had spent many summers when she was a girl and also to the ruins of Big Home,[24] so I wrote the

[23] Milford was built by Gov. John L. Manning in 1842 and was known locally as "Manning's Folly." (See below, page 54.)

[24] Big Home was probably built by Gen. R. C. Richardson. A description of it is given in an article in the *Columbia Record*, July 22, 1948, by Bernard Manning, grandson of Gov. R. I. Manning:

"The house at 'Big Home' had an avenue of over a mile of live oaks and huge bushes of gardenias. A large wing extended on each side of its front portico with great pillars. One of the wings was a great ballroom with a polished floor that rested on springs to give it an undulating motion. The other wing contained two immense bedrooms, each with a dressing-room opening onto a side piazza, belonging to the four daughters of the house. . . ."

The same article quotes from an unpublished manuscript by Elizabeth Allen Coxe (née Sinkler—the "Aunty" of this narrative) describing the marriage at Big Home of Norvell Richardson to her cousin John Peter Richardson December 3, 1869.

"It was at the Sand Hills home a very short distance from the pretty Gothic church which had no arangements for lights, so he (Mr. Richardson) had 18 Negroes dressed in burnouses like Moors, mounted on horses carrying torches. These horsemen rode by the carriages conveying the bridal party to the church and as there were 24 groomsmen and 24 bridesmaids . . . the procession was long and most picturesque. Then each man took his place outside one of the low pointed windows, holding his torch so as to give a flaming light inside the church, the chancel, of course, having many wax candles."

Belvidere: A Plantation Memory

present owners of Milford asking if we might drive up on a certain day and go over the grounds and the house. Though we did not know them, the reply was most cordial and hospitable.

We set forth after a rather early breakfast, Aunt Cad, Em, Nick, Cad [25] and I. We motored past freshly plowed fields where singing Negroes were at work and through a section which had been famous "before the war" for its great plantations and its splendid homes. Many of these houses had been burned and others were deserted or had disappeared. Thickets of wild plum were in bloom along the roadside with yellow jessamine in full flower climbing in them.

After a long drive, we stopped before a little house and asked a colored woman, who was bending over her washtubs under a big tree in the yard, if she could tell us where the road turned off which would take us to the ruins of Big Home and the Richardson family graveyard. She looked at us suspiciously, but when she was assured that we were some of the family she indicated a little path which ran through the fields into a thicket of woods and vines. Following this path we came suddenly upon the handsome monuments of General Richardson, his wife, Dolly and many other relatives of ours. Aunt Cad told us anecdotes of them all, one in particular of General Richardson. It was said that General Tarleton came storming up to Big

---

[25] "Em" and "Cad" are the author's sisters. "Nick" is Nicholas Guy Roosevelt of Philadelphia, husband of Em.

Home one day just after General Richardson had died and said to his wife, "Where is General Richardson?" She quietly replied, pointing to the graveyard, "He is where you cannot harm him." General Tarleton roared, "Have him dug up. I want to look on the face of the only man of whom I have ever been afraid."

Another story was that Cousin Jim Richardson, who lived at Mammus Hall and who was very fond of entertaining, had one evening put on a most unusual spectacle for his guests. He had all the lights in the house put out and suddenly the yard was a blaze of light from torches held by mounted Negroes, all in fancy dress. And into the open came eight young men, also in fancy dress, on handsome horses. The band struck up "The Lancers" and these wonderfully trained horses with their skillful riders went through the dance. Among these riders were Cousin Jim, himself, Dickie Richardson, Elliott Darby, Edward Brailsford, and others. Cousin Jim's band seems to have been a most remarkable one for it was made up of his own Negroes, all naturally gifted musicians, especially one Robin who could transpose the music to suit each piece.

Aunt Cad also told of a young cousin who showed no disposition to leave the shelter of his father's roof. When this young man reached his middle twenties, his father considered it high time for him to be taking wing from the home nest, so called him in, gave him five hundred dollars, wished him Godspeed and told him that when he had become permanently situated to write, giving his address and news of himself. There were tearful partings from mother, aunts, and sisters. All of the house servants came to see Young Maussa off; his dogs licked his hands in mournful realization that some family crisis was taking place. Finally the last kiss was given and the traveller dramatically departed. That evening about sunset there was heard the thud of hoofs and whirring of wheels and, amid the ecstatic barking of the dogs, a shiny new buggy drawn by a pair of flashy matched bays came whirling into the yard. The family all gathered, curious to see who their unexpected visitor was, and who should it prove to be but the son of the house. He had spent the entire five hundred on this outfit and returned to the bosom of the family which he never afterwards left.

From Big Home we drove on to Milford, locally known as "Manning's Folly." Here it was that Cousin John Manning had built a most magnificent house which he furnished with rare and beautiful things from the four corners of the earth. This place escaped the ravages of the war and it was sold intact, even to the monogrammed linens. It was said that later one Chinese vase from the house brought as much as the entire plantation had been sold for. Fortunately Milford was bought by some charming people from the West and used as a hunting preserve and winter home. They kindly showed us all over the house and grounds and listened to Aunt Cad's anecdotes of her girlhood summers there with great interest. It was altogether a successful and delightful day.

Belvidere: A Plantation Memory

Next April when Aunt Cad's visit was due, Em and I racked our brains as to what kind of party we could give her which would include a goodly number of the friends who always clamored to see her when she came south. We finally decided upon a barge party, despite Nick's doubts as to whether the older guests could negotiate the slippery canal banks. Em and I argued that if we chose an afternoon when the tide was high we could put planks directly from the bank to the barge and with the help of our two Negro oarsmen, Joe and Allen, get them all safely on board. Luckily we picked an afternoon of warm sunshine and gentle breezes. Everyone met at the Gippy Plantation [26] house, and from there, tucked in with cushions, rugs and tea baskets, we drove down to the rice fields. The drive through the swamp was lovely, for the afternoon sun shining through the green leaves which canopied the road gave a luminous light as though we were under water. Suddenly from this subdued light, we came out into the brilliant sunshine and there stretched before us were the rice fields with their flocks of chattering red-winged blackbirds and little marsh wrens swinging back and forth on the slender reeds. Against the distant smoky woods across the river, a few white herons were moving about, and occasionally we

[26] Gippy Plantation, once a part of the Fairlawn Barony on the western branch of the Cooper River, was so named after a local swamp where an old Negro named Gippy, an inveterate runaway, used to hide out in a hollow tree. The present owners are Mr. and Mrs. Nicholas G. Roosevelt of Philadelphia. Gippy is one of the plantations that has come most actively into new and useful life. Its upland fields are under crops of grain or serving as pastures for great flocks of sheep and a superb herd of Guernsey cattle. The old rice fields were, however, flooded by the Santee-Cooper waters.

saw a stately big blue heron stalking along the edges of the check-banks, hunting for little fish and frogs. We left the cars at Daddy Nat's cabin, passing the rice yard which was then swept clean and bare but which later in the season would be full of stacks of golden rice. When the rice was ripe, the cutters would go through the fields swinging their crescent blades, and the tiers would follow, bundling the cut grain into sheaves with amazing swiftness and skill. These bundles would then be carried along the check-banks to the waiting barge in the rice canal which would then float them to the rice yard.

    Our road now narrowed to a little path which ran along the top of the rice-bank to where Joe and Allen were waiting for us with the barge, or, as the Negroes call it, the "flat." They had spread clean rice straw over the floor and had put wide planks from one side to the other for seats which, with our blankets and cushions, did very well. There was a good deal of slithering and sliding but finally we all got on board without anyone falling in, to Nick's great relief. After we were seated, Joe and Allen took up the heavy, hand-hewn oars and eased us out into the canal toward the river. As the flat drifted slowly along, the green banks on either side were close enough for us to see all the wild flowers growing in lush abundance down to the water's edge, among them the dainty wild roses which dripped their fragile, pink faces in the ripples from the oars as we passed. Now and then we came to a silent figure sitting motionless on the bank smoking a pipe and fishing with a patience that only the colored people seem to possess. Sometimes the figure was that of a woman in soft faded calico dress and sometimes it was that of a man, but in either case it seemed to blend into the surroundings and to be a part of the warm brown earth which gives life to all things. The rice fields always seem to give one a sense of primal creation.

Presently the canal widened and soon we slipped out into the river itself which was at flood tide and so without current, its smooth surface making a perfect mirror to reflect the lazily drifting clouds and the tender blue sky. Little swallows were darting and swooping close to the surface and now and then a handsome kingfisher cut across the river at high speed and disappeared behind a tangle of wisteria vines on the farther bank. Occasionally a big blue heron would wing by, giving its characteristic croak, and one of our oarsmen would call after it, "All right, Po-Jo, ketch me a fish an' drap um to ma do'."

After an ample tea from our baskets, we settled comfortably on our cushions and urged Joe and Allen to sing for us, which, after an appropriate amount of demurring, they did. Their mellow voices rising in the plaintive and haunting old spirituals cast something of a spell upon us while the evening shadows deepened and the first stars appeared.

❈ IV ❈

IT is spring in the country that I seem to remember most vividly, but the fall and winter seasons likewise return to memory with a sharp sense of nostalgia. How fresh and lovely Belvidere looked, how clean and sweet it smelled after its early autumn scrubbing with lye and pine gum soap. When we returned to it after the summer months spent in the Pinelands, I sometimes wondered why we loved it so deeply and felt such special joy and contentment to be there. Life at the Pinelands was easy and pleasant and we had good times with our village friends there. But when the first "haad" frost came, blackening overnight the sweet potato vines and cotton leaves, we were always glad to be wakened by the sound of the wagons rolling into the yard to take us back to Belvidere.

Even with both houses furnished, we had much to move. The piano always went back and forth with us, and there was also a surprising amount of personal accumulation. Some of the family animals, including one of the milk cows, journeyed to and fro with us. Em had a single wagon all to herself to carry her potted plants, her flats of seedlings, and her coops of pet chickens which we all must help to capture the night before the move amid great cackling and squawking.

Papa always made sure that Mother had all the help needed, kissed her affectionately, and took off in his sulky. We would not see him again until we all sat down to an early hot supper at Belvidere. Mother and Mammy always left the Pinelands house last as they wanted to be sure all was in order and properly locked up. Then they clambered into the carriage with the table silver and various odds and ends in their laps and started off, driven, appropriately enough, by old Exodus, who by this time looked well nigh exhausted since he had been called on by everyone since early morn. As a child I used to feel a little conscience-stricken when I took a last look at the Pinelands house, so forlorn, closed up and deserted, for I felt that houses are like people and that this one must be wounded by our favoritism for the plantation. As we reached Belvidere, however, seeing the house waiting there at the head of the wide lawn, serene and lovely, I could feel nothing but a great surge of joy. I wished that I could give the whole place a hug and kiss for opening its gracious arms to us and saying "Welcome Home."

In the fall of the year especially the plantation hummed with life. Every evening wagons came creaking in from the fields piled high with cotton, chattering Negroes of all sizes and ages perched on top. From "the street" the busy puff, puff, puff of the gin was heard early and late. Daddy Major and his cohorts would bustle about with preparations for hog killing. There was always a crowd of little colored children playing outside Maum Rosena's gate and ever the sound of someone singing or laughing.

Christmas on the plantation was a great time for all, climaxed by our customary dinner for the colored children. Maum Rosena and Maum Margaret would cook this dinner in big iron wash pots in the yard. There were always two big pots of rice and one of "greens" that boiled for hours with fatback, and one of a rich goose, chicken and pork stew. An hour or more before sunset the children began to arrive, looking as though they had been scrubbed until they shone, all of them on their best behavior and armed with pans or tin plates and spoons. First helpings were eaten quietly and politely but when it was time for a second helping and the pots were getting low, all artificial notions of manners were dispensed with and spoons discarded. When the last morsels of rice and gravy had been stuffed into the greedy little mouths, cake and candy were handed out. What they could not eat at the moment, the diners tucked away in their pockets for future use. Then we would have games, songs, and dances, and soon "Ranky Tanky" and "Shortenin' Bread" were going strong, the smallest of the children singing all the words and keeping perfect time with feet and clapping hands, big eyes rolling, white teeth gleaming.

Plantation Negroes were, in general, carefree and well cared for under the old-style paternalistic system. The relationship of landowner and tenant was that of mutual

Belvidere: A Plantation Memory

dependence and satisfaction. The wheels of plantation life were kept turning by its Negro population; its profitable operation was only possible with their labor. On the other hand, the tenant's rent-free house was kept in good repair, garden land and housing for livestock were also free, and work was always available to him at fair wages. In sickness and in trouble his white people assumed responsibility for him and ministered to his needs.

My mother, known to all her devoted dependents as "Miss Annie," was a good, self-taught doctor and nurse. In the spring when there was an epidemic of "stomach complaint," I have seen her mixing peppermint, assafoetida, paregoric, and soda, in pitchers from which she filled the little bottles held by the colored women who were lined up at the side steps patiently waiting their turn. Later in the season when malaria stalked the plantation and almost every porch had a little Negro stretched out, generally on the floor, we were all pressed into service to help fill capsules with quinine powder and administer them to the sufferers. Many were the aches and miseries which Mother cured. As her patients said, "Miss Annie physic sho cut de pain." And many were the bowls of soup and other treats that were sent up to the sick on "the street" from the Big House kitchen.

There were spiritual as well as physical administrations. On Sunday afternoons, Miss Annie kept up the old custom of holding a Bible class in the church on the grassy hill in "the street." All ages came to these classes and hearty singing would alternate with the recitation in unison from memory of such Psalms as "The Lord is my Shepherd" or "I will lift up mine eyes unto the hills." Often I have heard Mother remind them that at the last day much would be required of them as they had had the opportunity of being taught and of knowing right from wrong.

After Mother was gone the colored community missed her sorely and its older members never ceased to grieve for her loss. Once when I went over to Belvidere from my own home in Pinopolis, Daddy Lewis met me with his face all lit up. "Oh, Miss Anne," he said, "Miss Annie bin yuh in the gaaden wid me yesterday an' talk wid me a good while an' she say she come to tell me I must stop fret after um, coz she cyan' res' long as I frettin' so hard. An' I tell um, 'Missis, I hafter fret after you, enty? coz I miss you too bad, but I try to do just like you say.' An' after we talk a while, she say, 'Lewis, I hafter go now,' and I walk wid um fur as de big pine and she say, 'Lewis, you cyan' come no furder wid me coz whay I'm goin' you cyan' come, not now.' An' I stand still an' watch um till she gone clean out of my sight!"

After Mother's death, Papa, who still lived at Belvidere, used to send for me from time to time to act as confidante, arbiter, or disciplinarian in the problems which so often arose. Once, for example, he wrote me to come up and have a talk with old Daddy Lewis who seemed troubled about something. When I reached Belvidere, I drove into the back gate which leads to the stable yard. As I reached Daddy Lewis' house he came out hat in hand, and after we exchanged the usual amenities he said, "Miss Anne, I sho glad you come yuh today, mam, cuz some debilment goin' on roun' dis plantation what I don' like none t'all. Lily she sho causin' a heap o' trouble on dis place. She dey in he house wid a raft o' chillun all roun' un an' not a husband to he name. Miss Anne, you know, dis is very haad on der young mans aroun' de plantation." I agreed, and hesitatingly, he went on that he was afraid that his son, William, had got "mixed up" with Lily and that Dorcas, his wife, was beginning to act up. I comforted him by telling him that I would talk to William and leaving him I sent word up "the street" by a little black, half naked boy to tell William to come down to the "big yard" as I wanted to see him.

It was a very warm afternoon and, as I wanted to have my talk with William away from the eager ears of the house servants, I had a chair put out in the yard and sat in the shade to wait for William to come. He arrived before long, looking very sheepish and hang-dog, and stood in front of me with his hat in his hand, shifting uneasily from one foot to the other. We went over the situation, and as best I could I brought home to him the humiliation he was causing his wife, Dorcas, and the worry to his old parents who had always held their heads so high. I told him that he was acting like any of the riff-raff and yahoos

Belvidere: A Plantation Memory

of the country instead of helping to uphold his family's good name and that of the plantation.

I had been talking so earnestly that I had not noticed an undercurrent of low murmurs, but at the end of our talk I glanced behind me and there, to my amazement and amusement, were a number of the colored people who had slipped quietly up from "the street." The men were squatting on their heels or leaning on trees and the women standing with their hands folded, as was their custom, under their aprons, all thoroughly enjoying the tongue lashing being administered to William. I heard one or two of them saying, "Miss Anne sho put it on him good dis time."

Maum Rosena was greatly loved by us and highly respected by all the Negroes on the plantation. One cold, gray January day in 1930, when I drove up to Belvidere to see Papa, I stopped in at Maum Rosena's on the way to the Big House to see how the old lady was. She had been sick for a long time and I was concerned about her. As I walked into the dim room, lit only by the flickering light of a sweet smelling cedar fire burning on the hearth, I noticed three or four figures sitting on low stools about the fire and I observed that Maum Rosena's bed had been turned so that the head of it was towards the open door leading out into the yard. There was a quilt over the back of the bed but a chill, penetrating draft was coming through the door. I did not protest, however, for I realized the watchers believed the end was near and they had opened the door and turned the bed so that the "chariot" would have no hindrance when it came and the spirit of the newly dead would be free to go. Maum Rosena was lying straight and still, her cheeks sunken and one thin hand lying motionless outside the patchwork quilt which was pulled up under her chin. As I stood there looking at her, memories of three generations of devoted service and friendship between her family and mine came over me and I was greatly saddened to think that she must leave us. A few weeks earlier when I had gone to see her, I found her sitting upright in bed, her tiny little body tense and a look of mysterious longing on her face. I went up and held her hand and spoke to her, but her mind was wandering and she did not know me. She kept peering around me at the open door and Liza told me she had been doing it all day. I wondered whether she was perhaps looking for her beloved "Miss Annie" or for Daddy Lewis.

Now after seeing that she was comfortable and that there was nothing I could do, I left her and went on to the house. In less than an hour Liza had come in to say that Maum Rosena had quietly slipped away. Maum Rosena's house was at the gate that leads from "the street" to the fields on the river, and for as far back as I can remember it was always running over with babies, toddlers, and small "nusses," for the women going out to work in the fields would drop their little ones with Maum Rosena on the way out and pick them up again in the evening on their way in—a free day-nursery for the plantation! And

Belvidere: A Plantation Memory

if any crowns are really given out in the next world, Maum Rosena will undoubtedly be wearing one of the brightest.

A death was of course a big social event on the plantation and marked by extensive ceremony. About a month after Maum Rosena's passing, I went up again to spend the week-end with Papa and noticed when old Exodus was helping me out of the car that his voice and manner indicated news to be imparted. Knowing that he would think it unsuitable to volunteer it, I asked how everyone on Belvidere was, and that gave him the opportunity to announce that Doc had died the previous night and that Julia was near distracted.

As it was already late, I did not go up "the street" to Julia's house but sent messages of condolence and an invitation to her to come down to the Big House in the morning to see me. Papa and I spent the evening talking before the fire in the parlor and at about eleven I went up to bed and immediately to sleep. A short time later, however, I gradually became aware that pushing up through my consciousness were sounds of distant singing, dull rhythmic beating, and a wailing which rose and fell. I struggled in my half-sleep to unravel these sounds and finally remembered Doc's death and knew that the whole colored population would be engaged in the "settin' up" which would go on till daybreak. There was something weird and disturbingly primitive in these voices drifting in on the night air, but I had, after all, heard the same thing many times so that it did not trouble me.

Belvidere: A Plantation Memory

Next morning when Liza came in to open the shutters and make the fire, the sun was up and I saw that it would be a beautiful day. As I stretched lazily in bed, I reflected that only in the south on a winter's morning would the red birds call back and forth to each other so sweetly and clearly. I asked Liza if she had stayed up all night at the "settin' up" and she replied that she had not been to bed at all but that biscuits and hot coffee had been handed around at three o'clock and that "had washed away the weariness."

Before I had time to get up there was a tap at the door and Julia entered. Her plump figure and habitually smiling face had fallen into lines of sorrow and she began at once to weep gently. I, of course, urged her to tell me the circumstances of Doc's death. First in most dramatic language she expressed her satisfaction that a short time before he had been "seekin'" and had come through mighty fine and been converted. Then on "night before las'," when she had not thought him very sick, he had wakened her and said he heard a far off rumbling which kept coming closer and closer. "'Baby,' he say, 'it mus be a train.' And I tell um, 'Doc, enty you know we ain got no train round yuh. And I don hear nuttin nohow.' An' he lay back down, but tereckly he sit up again an' he face all light up an' he say, 'Julia gal, lissen. Lissen, de rumblin' gittin closer and closer an' I know what it is now. It's de chariot! An' it comin' for me. Baby, I got to go now, gal.' An' he face all shine up an' he drap back. An' I call um and I

Belvidere: A Plantation Memory

say, 'Doc, Doc, can't you answer yo' baby?' An' he ain say nuttin, an' I know he done gone for true."

At this point Julia broke down and cried wildly. Then after a few minutes she said, "Missis, I had to let Doc insurance go, coz I ain't had de quarter a week to pay de man when he come roun'. I know you or the Gin'l would pay it for me if I had ax you, but you all two done do so much for Doc a'ready I ain had de heart to ax you."

But presently she wiped her eyes, brightened up and added, "Missis, I been in a heap o' trouble, but I got just one ting for t'ankful for. I keep a ten cent policy on Doc, so I gointa get somethin' off him anyhow."

The Low-country Negro is always polite, acquiescent, and anxious to please. I recall an excursion to Hampton, Archibald Rutledge's plantation, which Em, Nick, and I made one sunny December day. We chose a back road which leads through Hell Hole, Honey Hill, and other remote regions, and after an hour's drive found ourselves on unfamiliar, sandy roads which wound through apparently endless forests of big moss-draped pines. Another hour brought us no nearer Hampton and we decided to ask the first person we met for a little advice. This was much easier said than done as there was almost no one to ask. Houses were miles apart and those few we passed were set far back from the road in little clearings in the woods. Finally, however, we met two colored men with rifles over their shoulders. We stopped and Nick asked, "This the road to Hampton?" and they replied, "Yes, sir, Boss. Yes, sir. That's right, sir. Yes, sir," with deep bows and wide smiles. We drove on for another ten miles and still found ourselves deep in silent forests, mysteriously beautiful with shadows and soft blue haze. Just as we were discussing what to do, a tall Negro followed by the usual lean red hound turned into the road from a side path and I called to him, "Where does this road go?" The man replied readily, "Missis, where you want um for go?" "No," I said, "That isn't the point! *where does* it go?" The dwellers in these isolated, sparsely settled sections often have never been more than a few miles in any direction from their homes and are entirely ignorant of nearby places. This one thought over my question seriously and eventually produced with really courtly courtesy the answer, "Missis, dis road will take you mos' anywhere you want to go."

We thanked him and drove on, coming soon afterwards to a cross road along which was coming an ancient and dilapidated buggy drawn by a shaggy gray horse and driven by a very old man with white whiskers. As he approached, we watched with fascination the wheels of the buggy each going its own way and seemingly perilously near to dropping off. When the equipage drew up alongside our car, Nick very politely asked the ancient if he could direct us to Hampton Plantation. The old man cupped his hand behind his ear and, leaning out of his buggy, looked us all over inquiringly. So Nick tried again, this time shouting. The old fellow shook his head despondently but, reaching under the seat of the buggy, he brought forth a battered tin funnel which he put to his ear, remarking that he was "a leetle deef." By this time, Nick had got out of the car and, going up to the buggy, he took the edge of the funnel firmly in hand and bellowed into it. At once a broad smile spread over the weatherbeaten black face and the old man launched happily into detailed directions as to what turns should be taken to reach our objective, which was actually quite close by.

We were soon driving up to the stately and beautiful house that had been the home of the Rutledges for many generations and which Archibald Rutledge has immortalized in many delightful stories of his boyhood days there, of the animal life in the nearby swamps, and of the colored people who were always an important part of the Hampton scene.

❋ V ❋

SAMUEL DuBOSE, in his *Reminiscences of St. Stephen's Parish*, describes travel conditions in the decades which followed the Revolution:

In my boyhood, there was not a four-wheeled carriage owned, in that part of Santee which I have been describing with the exception of a heavy and unsightly vehicle, something like a baggage wagon, owned by General Marion. It was called a Caravan, and was drawn by four horses, ridden by postillions. . . . About the year 1800 carriages became more common. Without being more commodious than those now in use, they were very costly and heavy. Every panel had a glass and venetian blinds, they generally cost a thousand dollars and required to be drawn by four horses.[27]

Although vehicles had improved by Grandpa's time, travel was still slow and difficult. In much later years when we motored along the highways at 50 miles an hour Aunt Cad was wont to point out the contrast in transportation over the same routes in her girlhood days.

[27] Samuel DuBose, *Reminiscences of St. Stephen's Parish*, p. 30.

"A drive which now takes only a few hours was an undertaking then—and an adventure—which sometimes lasted several days" she said. Here is the story of one such journey as she told it to us.

Sister Lizzie and I had just returned from a grand trip to Europe and when I got back to Belvidere, Papa thought he would take me to see dear Aunt Eliza Manning who lived across the river and swamp, about forty or fifty miles as the crow flies. We got there by a circuitous route on a laborious little 'shoo-fly' train and had a happy little visit. When the day came to start home, Papa planned to send me back by the same little train and return himself by horseback through the swamp, but I begged hard to go with him and he finally agreed. We learned that if we could get to Wright's Bluff we could catch a river boat which carried cotton up and down the Santee, so we drove down about thirty miles to where a cousin lived and spent the night. The following morning we had to start out on a bitter cold dawn, driving fifteen miles in a curious buckboard wagon before we reached the steamer landing. As we drew near there was a foreboding sense of silence and to our dismay we found that the boat had left and that there would be no other trip for a week, or perhaps for two weeks as the schedule was very erratic. We now realized we would either have to drive back to the Mannings or take our chance of getting through the swamp to the ferry. Our host kindly arranged for us to have a spirited horse and an excellent Negro driver, so, nothing daunted, we decided to go on in the buckboard.

I shall never forget the beauty of the swamp on that drive—the great, towering trees, the deep shadows, and eery stillness. The road was extremely narrow, mostly just a causeway with deep ditches on either side. The water in the road was frozen over and as we went on the horse became wilder and wilder and became frightened by the breaking ice beneath his feet and the crunching sound of the wheels in the frozen ruts. He finally refused to budge any further, either with coaxing or whipping, and made a succession of balks and lunges which almost turned us over. Papa decided that there was nothing to do but go back to the edge of the swamp and get an old hunter, Daddy Stephen, who lived there, to bring his mules and help us out. He managed to get the temperamental horse out of the shafts and, assuring me that he would be back as soon as possible, mounted and disappeared in the forest. The driver and I were by this time cowering with cold, sitting disconsolately in the buckboard which was standing hub deep in the icy water. The Negro, feeling that I was in his charge, valiantly tried to entertain me with stories of bygone days. I asked his name and he answered, 'Miss Carrie, they calls me Hardy Hard Times, but my real name is James Nathan Simon Hampton.' I gave him all my lunch and told him to try to get down out of the wagon, which he succeeded in doing, eventually managing to start a little fire by which he warmed himself.

Every now and then a stray hunter would come through the swamp and pause to talk to us from the bank, but it became colder and colder and seemed increasingly lonely. At last, to my intense relief, we could hear hallooing in the distance, and after a while Papa and Daddy Stephen appeared, Papa riding another horse and Daddy Stephen a mule. After considerable difficulty the mule was hitched to the buckboard and we started on our way again, passing through some superb forest and fording some very cold creeks. Finally, towards dusk, we got to the bank of the river itself, and there we built bon-fires hoping to attract the attention of the people on the other side and get a 'flat' to pole us across, but apparently there was no one on the far bank for we could not see a sign of life. We kept the bon-fire going, however, and occasionally a hunter would appear and stray cattle, wintering in the swamp, would wander up to investigate. After waiting for some while with no response from the other side of the river, we concluded to go along the river for four or five miles which wuld bring us opposite Sinkler's landing.

When finally we got there, we could hear through the dark the barking of dogs and the sound of wood chopping from "the street" at Belvidere, so near and yet so far. Daddy Long Robert had a house quite near the landing so Papa and Daddy Stephen started whooping and calling until a window was flung open and a stream of light poured out across the swift flowing river. A woman's voice called "Who dat?" and Daddy Stephen hollered back, "Lavinia, dat you? Tell Robert dat Maussa an' Miss Carrie ober here an' bring de bateau for carry dem to de udder side." To our dismay Lavinia cried out "Who dat call my name out de swamp? It's Treefoot callin' my name an' I ainter gwine to listen." With that the window banged shut and we were left in darkness again.

At least an hour later Daddy Long Robert himself came home, saw our fire across the river and shouted to us, and before long his bateau slid up to the mud bank near us. After grateful farewells to Daddy Stephen and Hardy, we were soon safely across the river and home at Belvidere. It had taken us two days and a night to get there from the Mannings! I was dressed in my new French clothes, unsuited to such an excursion, but I was young and so considered it all an exciting episode.

Horse-and-buggy days lasted in the country for a long while after Aunt Cad's girlhood. A letter to me from Laura Stevens in the spring of 1907 gives a graphic description of a typical 12-mile drive and, incidentally, a picture of the plantation section traversed by our local roads.

Lewisfield
Sunday night

Dearest Anne:

This can only be a short letter as our monthly drive to Strawberry Church[28] *leaves us physically exhausted. As*

---

[28] Strawberry was built in 1752 as a Chapel-of-Ease to Biggin Church, this being a chapel erected close to the center of the Parish population so that in bad weather the congregation would not have to drive so far over bad roads to the main church.

you know, we go to Pinopolis three Sundays as at Strawberry there is a visiting rector from Charleston only once a month. It is a pilgrimage! But Papa makes it very interesting telling us anecdotes of the thirteen plantations that we traverse, nearly all of them now deserted and some of them burned. And of course these drives are an adventure on account of the roads.

We left Lewisfield at 10 hoping to get to the Ferry by 12 o'clock. Cousin Fan and several others are with us, so six of us drove in the high yellow-wheel carriage with Nellie and Togo, and Sister and a beau drove our spryest mule in the buggy. At Mulberry Castle[29] a double-buggy full of Porchers joined the cavalcade and we proceeded at a very good pace through South Mulberry and Harry Hill where there must have been at one time a garden tenderly cared for and loved. The Porchers and ourselves drive there every March and pick the loveliest long-stemmed jonquils and look longingly at the old shrubs.

After turning into Dockon and driving down the beautiful avenue, the road on the other side of Wappacolah[30] is so full of pitfalls that at intervals the men have to pry up the wheels of the buggies to get us out of mud holes.

[29] The Mulberry was built in 1714 by Thomas Broughton who modeled it after Seaton Hall, the ancestral home of the Broughtons in England. This is one of South Carolina's most beautiful and famous places.

[30] Wappacolah was built about 1800. The plantation was the inheritance of Henrietta Wragg and later came into the possession of Francis William Heyward who in 1873 married the noted beauty Frances Ferguson of the adjoining Dockon Plantation.

Belvidere: A Plantation Memory

Then, as you remember, comes the Bluff[31] *and the horseshoe avenue of liveoaks leading up to the Pimlico*[32] *house. When we finally reached the Strawberry Ferry*[33] *we found the ever faithful Heywards already there waiting. The horses were unhitched and tied to trees and we all whooped for old Daddy Si to bring the flat boat over for us. He was very slow as usual, but we were not a bit uneasy about being late, as service cannot start without us as we are half of the congregation. Mama of course continued her knitting as she does on all occasions.*

Finally the flat arrived and we were ferried over and landed at Rice Hope and walked up the cedar lined road to the darling little brick and plaster church nestled under the giant liveoaks. Papa was horrified to find that some of his hounds had followed us and was even more dismayed to see them swimming behind the flat boat when we were crossing the river for he hoped they would at any rate stay with the horses. As it was a very warm spring day and alligators are plentiful at this season and have a special fondness for dog meat, when we reached the church Papa insisted on bringing the hounds inside and shutting the doors so that they could not get into trouble. They made an

[31] The Bluff was a plantation acquired by Dr. William Moultrie, the fourth eminent physician in direct descent from the emigrant Dr. John Moultrie, by his marriage to Hannah Harleston in 1826.

[32] Pimlico was one of the six tracts into which the Mepshew plantation of James Colleton was divided when it was sequestered and sold by the State after the Revolution.

[33] Strawberry Ferry crossed the western branch of the Cooper River opposite The Bluff plantation. It was established by an act of the Assembly in 1705 and has been in operation until recent years. One can still see faintly on a plank attached to a nearby tree, the ferry fare marked in shillings.

unusual addition to the congregation but behaved quite well on the whole and the congregation and minister took them in their stride.

We are all looking forward to our spring visit to Belvidere next week. We love the drive from Lewisfield through Middle and Upper St. Johns, reaching Belvidere at sunset with the mingled smells of sweet olive, wood smoke and baking ham to geet us, and old Daddy Tom coming from the kitchen to the house with a big tray of hot supper under the pewter covers balanced on his shoulder.

We must do lots of reading aloud and walking, and I thirst for my revenge at backgammon.

Till next week then, and lots of love
Baby

Because getting from one place to another took considerable time, the numerous parties which enlivened life for plantation young people were frequently all day affairs. During our summers in the Pinelands one of these which we most enjoyed was a picnic-dance at The Rocks.[34] Such a day would begin early for Em and me with Mammy bringing up buckets of cold water from the cistern for our baths, waking us with her usual injunction of "Arise, Virgins," and laying out our muslin or dimity dresses while we hurried in and out of the tin tubs. Soon our escorts arrived in a buggy, Em and I and our baskets of lunch were

[34] The Rocks was built in 1800 by Capt. Peter Gaillard of White Plains Plantation, St. Stephen's Parish. Captain Gaillard was the son of the Huguenot emigrant of that name and was born at Wambaw Plantation, St. James' Parish, in 1757.

tucked into place and presently we were trotting along the sandy ruts of the "Big Road" which runs through the village. As we passed the rambling roads leading up to various village houses, buggies joined us and dropped into line until there was a procession of us, all heading towards the River Road and the plantation country. Along the side of the road there would be big white mallows blooming, clumps of black-eyed-Susans, and bushes of lacy feverflower, so called by the Negroes because it blooms during the malarial season. There were also quantities of rabbit peas and bright orange butterfly weed, and bracken.

We would often have to turn aside for wagons full of Negroes who were going to Eutawville to buy their week's "grocery," a few yards of bright chambray, plugs of tobacco, and other necessities. Some of these wagons had chairs set in them for the women-folk who wore stiff starched white aprons over their cotton dresses. They would fan themselves with palmetto fans as the wagon slowly bounced and creaked along, and of course a great deal of laughing and talking went on. If it was a chilly day, likely as not a little smoke would be seen coming from the middle of these wagons as it was customary to place a piece of tin holding a bed of coals on the floor to warm the leisurely traveller.

When we passed out of the Pinelands we came to broad open fields of blooming cotton and tasselled corn. Moss-hung oaks took the place of the pines and we seemed to be driving through miles of stately avenues. At last we turned in at the gates of The Rocks and drew up in the shade of its great trees. While the men unhitched the horses and tied them the girls carried the lunch to the coolest end of the piazza and made buckets of lemonade. Cousin Margie,[35] who always chaperoned us, would settle herself comfortably in a rocker in the open doorway of the house where she could keep cool and at the same time overlook house, piazzas, and lawn. Cousin Peter and Cousin Eugene Gaillard[36] brought out their fiddles and soon had us all dancing to the tune of "Sharem, don' keer how you sharem, jes so you sharem even." Cousin Peter and Cousin Eugene were alike in their love of young people and their willingness to join in our parties and fiddle for us all day, or all night, as the case might be.

Some of the guests, from time to time, added a mouth organ, another fiddle or a guitar to the orchestration and we would dance almost without intermission until dinner time; then all the baskets of good things to eat were unpacked and everyone fell to with gusto. After dinner we rested for a while, the girls sitting together under the trees on the buggy blankets and the men smoking and chatting together about crops, politics, and live-stock. Then some of us had dates for strolls, or paddles on the lake, and some of us flirted in the garden, but when the fiddles called us back to the house the dance was on again in full swing. Before dusk Cousin Pete would start playing "Home Sweet

[35] Margaret Sinkler Gaillard of Eutaw.

[36] Peter and Eugene Gaillard were sons of Eugene and Camilla Gaillard of Hayden Hill Plantation.

Home," as it was considered dangerous in summer to linger on the plantations after sunset on account of the malarial mosquitoes. So we collected the baskets and closed in the heavy shutters while the men were hitching up the buggies again. Then we were trotting back towards the Pinelands, but not so fast that we could not notice the heavy sweetness of blooming wild grape in the evening air and the sound of the "Chuck-will's-widows" calling to each other across the fields.

❊ VI ❊

THE greatest event of my girhood to date was the wedding at Lewisfield in November, 1908, of Elizabeth Stevens to Alexander Martin of Virginia. Liz was the first of all of us girls to be married and we would naturally have been greatly excited over it even if it had been a far less festive occasion. But invitations had been sent to all the relatives and friends not only in the South but in the North as well and a special car was to be added to the regular evening train from Charleston for the wedding guests from "town."

Our Belvidere household, white and colored, had been asked to come several days ahead to help with preparations and decorations. Mother had made a large fruit cake and quarts of her famous wine jelly, molded in one of the old Belvidere stone molds which has fluted sides and a bunch of fruit and flowers on the bottom, making any dessert which is turned out of it look as pretty as it tastes good. Daddy Lewis had washed and polished the carriage and shined the brasses on the harness until they shone like gold in the sunshine. The gray mares, Papa's pets, had been curried and brushed until they were sleek as satin; trunks had been packed and loaded, and finally our cavalcade drove through the Belvidere gates and set out on the long journey to Lewisfield.

The carriage headed the procession, and alongside rode Daddy Lewis on a mule, going along as always for the first couple of miles so that Papa could give him last directions as to what was to be done in his absence. Then came the "spring wagon" with all the luggage, extra saddles and guns and Mammy perched beside the driver in her stiff-starched white apron, the inevitable "fascinator" wound around her head under her hat. And lastly, some distance behind, came my bay mare, Ladysmith, and me.

We had arranged to meet at "Percy's Store" for lunch. The road was rough and we therefore had to go slowly, but also, as the Negroes expressed it, "the Ginral don't like to rush he creetur." The drive between the two plantations always took most of a short winter day and it was a welcome break to everyone to stop and unhitch the horses, spread out the carriage blankets on the side of the road in the sun and spend an hour eating lunch and relaxing.

Em always got bored early on the journey and customarily supplied herself with reading matter in which she buried herself for hours at a time in spite of the jouncing of the carriage. This made her rather an unsatisfactory travelling companion.

This particular trip was slower than usual for on account of recent rains we had to slosh through long flats of shallow brandy-colored water. Gradually, however, we reached and passed our familiar landmarks—the Soldier's Grave, the house of Daddy Gibby Nelson from whom Grandpa always used to buy shuck collars for his mules; then Chapel Hill, Ophir, the entrance to Northampton of many childhood memories, Cedar Spring, Brunswick, and White Hall Plantations.[37] By the time we reached the Lewisfield swamp it was dark, and after crossing this it was with pleasure and relief that we saw ahead of us the lights of the big house, and rising over the low rice fields beyond and shining on the river, a big full moon.

The minute we arrived there was a rush of hurrying feet, doors banged open, and in a minute we were inside by the big fires all talking at once and drinking Uncle's famous cherry bounce.

During the next few days the house became fuller and fuller hourly, as more and more relatives came to stay. In addition to the table in the dining room which had been opened to its full length, there were tables on the piazza where the young people had meals. I don't see how Greaty and Uncle fed us all but there seemed to be a never-ending supply of sausages, game of all kinds and delicious fish, fresh from the river.

[37] Ophir was settled by Peter Porcher of Peru Plantation about 1770.
Cedar Spring was built in 1804 by George Porcher.
Brunswick, formerly a St. Julien plantation, was afterwards owned by the Ravenel and Peyre families.
White Hall was built about 1824 by Thomas Porcher of Ophir for his son Thomas who married Catherine Gaillard, daughter of Peter Gaillard of The Rocks.

These days before the wedding flew gaily by and at last the great day dawned, brilliant and mild. The wedding was to take place at eight in the evening and at sunset big bonfires were lit along the road through the swamp. About this time the bridesmaids (of which I was one) were sent upstairs ostensibly to rest, in any case not to be seen until we burst upon the assemblage in all our finery. Liz was put into her room with only her maid of honor and Maum Kat who was told to let no one come in to disturb her missy until time to dress. I can see 225-pound Maum Kat now, dressed in vivid watermelon-colored chambray, stiff-starched white apron and head "hankercher," and wearing great gold hoop earrings, seated firmly on the floor with her back against Liz's door, proud that no one could move her without help of a derrick.

At last the time came for us to dress and we all exclaimed with delight as the misty white net dresses and white satin slips, made for us in Philadelphia by Madame Vibaux, Auntie's own dress-maker, were lifted out of their tissue paper. When we were ready to go down, eight lovely silver roses, one for each bridesmaid to wear in her hair, were brought in as a gift from the bride. When these were arranged we all collected at the head of the broad stairway. Below stood Cousin Richard Manning with a list of the bridesmaids and groomsmen in his hand. As he called out our names, we went down and were joined by our groomsmen. At this moment, the strains of the wedding march came floating down the hall, the parlor doors were thrown open, and we marched in, a-tremble with excitement. An altar had been made at the far end of the parlor and a silver ribboned aisle, dividing the guests, led the full length of the room to it. Here, under garlands of smilax and river holly, Liz was married to Alex.

Afterwards there was a big supper and quantities of beverages of all kinds from champagne to plain whiskey were served, and many were the amusing incidents which took place.

After some of the guests had gone, the crowd thinned enough for dancing to start. It continued until the early hours of the morning when most of us were glad to crawl into our beds. However, as I was about to fall asleep I began to hear queer clattering noises and smothered laughter. Tiptoeing to the door, I saw one of the groomsmen who had been billeted in the attic come sliding down the curved stairway on a tin tray, landing with a crash in the hall. At once every door on the hall opened and out came startled or curious persons in various stages of undress. A Philadelphia guest inquired plaintively, "Do Southerners ever sleep?" Not, she was answered, on a night like this!

After this there were other family weddings at Lewisfield and Belvidere. One of greatest importance, which illness prevented me from attending, was that of my sister Emily and Nicholas G. Roosevelt of Philadelphia. Caddie's letter describing it, however, gives a very colorful and clear picture of it.

Belvidere Plantation
April 15, 1916

Dearest Sister Anne:

I promised to be your eyes for Sister's wedding so without further lamentations on your bitterly deplored absence, here goes.

The morning of April 15 dawned warm and clear, and the hush of the quiet house was broken almost as sharply as in Tennyson's description of the breaking of the spell in "The Sleeping Beauty"— "There rose a sound of striking clocks and feet that ran and crowing cocks. . . ."

The day gathered momentum rapidly. Mother in her quick, quiet voice giving a dozen orders, answering a hundred questions and dealing with each new crisis as it arose with unruffled authority. People, black and white, streamed into the yard, bringing presents of live chickens, eggs, beat pindar, flowers. Servants and their hordes of friends needing to be directed, calmed, hastened; messengers on horseback and in Fords demanding attention. Dinner was eaten and over, and things happened faster and faster until Nick and Howard Henry arrived from Eutaw. It was time for the bridesmaids to dress and the last pause before the storm was upon us.

The colored people had been arriving by wagon and buggy, mule and horse, until the street was alive with them. Then up the front drive the white guests began to arrive. The procession was led by Cousin Julia Greenwood (who, as you remember, married an Englishman and lives *in Gibralter) in a taxi which arrived too late to get her to the train and which was thereupon commandeered by her for the 60 mile drive! She managed it by sheer force of personality and, having won that round, it was easy to keep her kidnapped taxi driver at her preferred pace of 30 miles per hour and in the plumb middle of the road and—as you may imagine—she was followed by the maddest, dustiest lot of motorists you ever saw.*

Cousin Anna Sinkler drove over from Eutaw and had the smartest turn-out of all. Winnie Davis' coat gleaming like satin and the little high-wheeled cart polished to the nines. "Our boys" (Gaillards, Simons, Kirks) did the Low Country credit and the neighborhood turned out. I never did fathom how all the northerners got there but there were lots of ritzy-looking cars and a great many Charleston friends took the long drive. Wasn't it lovely to have the Mannings! Cousin Richard,[38] so handsome and every inch the Governor. Also Nick's Uncle Sam Roosevelt, the artist, added a distinguished note with his foreign-looking beard.

Well, here it is, the big moment! and you can picture the lawn bathed in soft April sunshine, the old cedars casting their long shadows. An aisle opened up between the guests from the front steps to the big live oak, and there was Bishop Guerry, benign and imposing in the enormous white muslin sleeves and robes of his office, and Mother

---

[38] Richard Irvine Manning, son of Col. R. I. Manning and Elizabeth Allen Sinkler Manning, was born in 1859 at Homesley, Sumter County. He was planter, banker, State senator, and from 1915 to 1919, governor of South Carolina.

walking down on Cousin Richard's arm to take her place. Then little Charles Kollock and your little Em soberly walked to the end of the white carpet, followed by the bridesmaids on the arms of the ushers. They looked particularly pretty in the simplest sheer white, with robins-egg blue sashes and bouquets of pink roses, (Henrietta, Harriott, Carrie, Mell and Elsie). Then me, in ruffled robins-egg taffeta; and then Papa, very dignified in plum-colored velveteen, with Sister, radiantly beautiful. Nick and Howard appeared as if by magic to meet them or, as Austin put it, they just dropped out of the live oak. The ceremony was soon over and everyone swept up to the steps where the bride and groom stood with the sweet olive in full bloom for a back drop. In a twinkling, tables and chairs were set out, waiters, champagne, and food appeared, and the woods and lawns bloomed with the gaily colored dresses of the women. . . .

The shadows lengthened, the white guests took their departure, and the colored gathered together and sounds of their laughter and chatter drifted down from the street. The Roosevelts got away amidst the proper confusion with a cortege of cars careening around the curve and out of sight in the deepening twilight. . . .

It was a shame you couldn't be there to enjoy it all. Get well soon, and lots of love.

Your devoted
Caddie

❋ VII ❋

THE Santee Jockey Club began its activities in 1791. On a course at Pineville, races were held for more than sixty years and drew large crowds, and until the beginning of the Confederate War the Club encouraged the breeding, training, and showing of fine horses in the sports-loving plantation community. It was revived in 1936 under the name of the St. John's Jockey Club by the descendants of the earlier enthusiasts and a sandy turf course was built at Belvidere. The Thanksgiving Races of that year were the first of a series run semi-annually thereafter over the five-eighths-mile track.

The interest in thoroughbreds dates back to early colonial times in Berkeley County. As early as 1749 importations of blooded stock were being made from England and by 1761 Daniel Ravenel of Wantoot was breeding thoroughbreds on a commercial basis. Peter Sinkler of Lifeland also raised blooded stock on a large scale and the Sinklers of Belvidere and Eutaw likewise bred and trained race horses which were locally famous.

At the Jockey Club races one seldom, if ever, found a professional race horse. Many were thoroughbreds but most of them were horses used in one way or another on the plantations to which they belonged. The racing meets gave the owners an opportunity to share their common interest in an atmosphere of good sportsmanship and spirited competition.

After the opening meet in late November, 1936, a great many letters of congratulation came to Belvidere. DuBose Heyward wrote

> *... I was amazed at what the community had accomplished and I cannot tell you how proud and pleased I was at the vitality of our dear old countryside. There was a lack of professional sporting atmosphere, a return to the simple natural sport for gentlemen that must have been of the very essence of the ante-bellum racing that our "grands" knew. It warmed my heart.*

I recall most vividly the details of that first race day, one which set the pattern for others to follow. In the early morning, a steady drumming sound pulled me out of deep sleep and subconsciously along with it was an uneasy sense of foreboding. Half-awake, I recognized the sound as rain falling steadily on the roof and abruptly I was jerked into full consciousness of its significance. This was race day and it was raining! At this moment there was a tap on the door and Dick came in with his face reflecting heaviest gloom. Sitting on the edge of the bed, he wailed, "Cousin Anne, what are we going to do? It's been raining all night and it's still pouring. We can't put off the races because we can't get word around. The roads will be like soup; people won't know what to do; half will come and half won't and it will be the most awful mess and flop!"

While Dick was listing his worries as President of the St. John's Racing Club, my mind ran to my personal troubles. I thought of the big house filled to overflowing with family and friends, of the turkeys and hams which had been roasted the previous day; of the mounds of stuffing and quarts of gravy, the bowls of tomato jelly, the quantities of cakes and cookies—all waiting in the old brick "meat room" for the expected guests. Searching for a word of comfort, all I could find was the old adage of "Rain before seven, clear before eleven," upon which I advised Dick to go down to the kitchen and get from Julia a big cup of strong black coffee.

Soon there were sounds of awakening and stirring in the house, doors opening and closing, the fragrance of steaming coffee being carried through the halls, the smell of lightwood as fires were lit in the bedrooms. At about 9:30 we were all at breakfast, enjoying Julia's corn cakes and waffles and trying not to mention the weather when, looking out of the window, I noticed the gold race horse weathervane which Uncle Wharton had given to the plantation many years ago slowly but surely swinging around to the west. The old people say that for the weather to change and set fair the wind has to go around the long way, but we didn't care whether it stayed fair or not so long as it cleared for race day. We rushed to the window and looked out hopefully. Sure enough, the rain had stopped and here and there patches of blue showed through the lifting clouds. Presently, with dramatic suddenness the sun burst out, and with equal suddenness house and stable yards were automatically galvanized into action. Aprons were tied on, apples and stalks of celery by the dozen were cut into salad, hams and turkeys were brought from the meat room and carving began. Colored boys dashed in and out.... "Cap sez, please mam, whey you put de flags?" ... "Marse Dick say please mam sen' him de numbers for de saddle cloths."

By noon all was ready. The girls had decorated the luncheon table beautifully with an enormous pumpkin scooped out and cut like a basket and filled with fruits, bunches of grapes, and sprays of the coral bush blooming in the yard, and around it produce from our fields was banked, half-shucked ears of red and yellow corn, polished yams, and white cotton bolls. If ever a table could be said to groan under the weight of its food, this one could, and, as the first cars of guests drove up, piping hot macaroni pies and candied sweet potatoes were brought in and added to the cold dishes. The house was soon filled with friends, laughing, talking, drinking healths, kissing kin, and exchanging tips on the races. A mint julep had been mixed in a large silver loving cup and this was passed around amid much back-slapping and exchange of reminiscences. Old Cousin Theodore Ravenel was very much in evidence when the cup was passed and took it as an opportunity to kiss soundly every girl within reach.

At 1:30 Dick warned everybody that he was going to start the races on the stroke of two and as quickly as the house had filled before lunch, it now emptied and we all hurried over to the race track with servants and colored children hanging on the running boards of family cars. The first view of the track with the surrounding whitewashed fence, the bright green oval, the red and white flags whipping in the breeze, brought a lift of excitement and pleasure to the heart. Beyond were the gay crowds of spectators and over to one side under the pines were the horses being led about by stable boys, their shining coats glistening in the sun and their pointed ears nervously twitching.

For the Belvidere family, the day was crowned by the fact that our own "Will Rogers," bred and raised by us, won the feature race, in reward for which he was given a bottle of Coca Cola which he dearly loved, and his jockey, Cogburn Gaillard, got a hug and kiss from me before the whole crowd. This, however, was not as much enjoyed as the Coca Cola.

After the races, the crowd thinned rapidly. Many Charleston friends headed for Gippy Plantation where Em and Nick were having a big buffet supper; horses were loaded into trucks and trailers, private debts were settled and last toasts exchanged. When I got back to the house, I found a number of friends had preceded me there and coffee and cake was soon passed around.

Belvidere: A Plantation Memory

That night before going to bed, I walked out on the open piazza and stood for a moment to enjoy the sharp, clean night air, listening to the sounds of the plantation. From the colored street came the sound of wood-chopping, a dog barking, an occasional laugh. But what was that other sound? Was it imagination, or the wind in the trees? No, I knew what it was. I knew it was the drumming of the hooves of the Sinkler horses of long ago sweeping around the curve into the home stretch.

❈ VIII ❈

A CANAL had been cut from the Santee River to the Cooper as early as 1800, traversing 22 miles of the fertile plantation country of lower Carolina and providing portage for the rich yields of rice, indigo, corn and cotton to the port of Charleston. Canal barges were pulled by mules using a 10-foot tow path along its green and flowery banks, carrying produce of all kinds from plantation to plantation, from little town to village, and finally to the state's export terminal. Early records show that in the year 1830 alone more than seventeen hundred boats arrived in Charleston by way of the Santee Canal bringing eighty thousand bales of cotton. The Charleston *Times* of May 29, 1801, featured this bit of promotional optimism:

We are happy to announce that Mr. William Buford who lives on the banks of the Broad River near Pinckney Courthouse (92 miles above Columbia) arrived in this city on Tuesday 26th with his own boat built on his own land and loaded with his own crop. With further improvements to the tributaries of the Santee, the superabounding products of the upper country will flow into Charleston in such full tides and with so much expedition and so little expense, as will lower our markets, and at the same time fill the pockets of our remote fellow citizens.

But by 1850 the canal had to be abandoned as a commercial waterway. Droughts, the completion of the railroad to Charleston, and other factors operated disastrously against it, and eventually it fell into disuse. As a child I remember one of the old locks, lined with bricks said to have been brought over from England, its gates, set in marble pivots, overgrown with wild grape, trumpet and jessamine vines. Our old great-uncle Mazyck Porcher used to tell us of sitting on his piazza at Mexico Plantation on spring evenings watching the barges passing along the canal at the foot of his lawn and hearing the songs of the Negro mule drivers.

Imagination clothed the old waterway with a special picturesqueness. But more than that, the engineering possibilities of a link between the Santee and the Cooper Rivers fired the interest of successive groups of progressive citizens. With the passing years physical evidences of the first canal were obscured, but the 35-foot natural drop from one river to the other at this point was not forgotten and twentieth century promoters were strongly attracted by the tremendous potentialities for electric power. Thus the Santee-Cooper hydro-electric power project came into being and construction was eventually started on giant dams, locks, and power citadels, close by the location of the earlier canal and locks. The lands lying in the natural basins for the two vast reservoirs were doomed, for the enterprise demanded it. This meant the flooding of thousands of fertile acres, the clearing of many square miles of timber, and the uprooting and re-settling of hundreds of families, many of whom had owned and loved their dwelling places through many generations. It also meant the obliteration of various historic sites.

A casualty of the lower reservoir was Northampton, home of General Moultrie, friend of George Washington, governor of the state and first president of the Santee Canal Company which was chartered in 1786. During our visits to the Stevens family who lived there during my childhood, we became familiar with nearby plantations also in the area to be flooded—Hanover, Woodlawn, Ophir, Somerset, Bunker Hill, White Hall. Water impounded by the upper Santee dam condemned The Rocks, Pond Bluff, Mt. Pleasant—and Belvidere.

When our neighborhood heard the news that the "project" had actually been passed and funds allocated for the building of the dam, we felt stunned and stricken. We had consoled ourselves during the long months when the matter was in controversy with the hope that sufficient money would never be available or that, due to the many limestone sinks leading to underground streams, the engineers would find that the "basin" would not hold water, and that through some such obstacle the whole undertaking would have to be dropped. It seemed incredible, impossible, that it could happen.

Belvidere: A Plantation Memory

Fortunately the older members of our family and, with a few exceptions, the older generation of our faithful colored people had passed into the Great Beyond and so were spared the sorrow and upheaval. For there came, inexorably, the sad and dreadful day when we began dismantling the house, a large house filled with the countless possessions collected by generation after generation to whom it was home—books brought from Italy, handsomely bound in white calf and scrolled in gold; a Chinese teakwood cabinet full of rare and romantic souvenirs, among them an exquisitely carved red and white ivory chess set brought home from his travels by a young midshipman member of the family in the early 1800's; portraits, pictures, silver, china, glass, linen, furniture, rugs, kitchen equipment, books without number, odds and ends of small material value, but priceless from association and part of the web and woof of happy recollection.

At last after many weary weeks the job was finished and it was as though a cruel hand had torn out the strings of a great harp which had been producing music, sometimes sad, sometimes joyous, but always worth hearing, for nearly a hundred and sixty years. The rooms had been swept clean and bare, each servant connected with the house had been given mementoes, and there remained only Papa's portrait over the parlor mantel still to be taken down. A truck waited at the foot of the brick steps for it and groups of colored people stood about, dramatically conscious of the occasion. As the portrait was brought out of the house and put on the truck, a hush fell on the group and then a low moaning broke out among the women, for it was as though this was the final page of a story ended forever.

The colored population of Belvidere at this time numbered about one hundred and eighty-five, some living in small white-washed houses in "the street" and some in comfortable little settlements on the banks of the Santee which ran through the lower part of the plantation known as "Dorchee." I am glad to say that we were able to re-settle all of these families on some pinelands belonging to Belvidere that were not flooded and which they affectionately call "Little Belvidere." Here they are reunited, close to their old haunts and familiar surroundings, near to friends and church. Lumber from the old houses built the new ones, bricks from the Big House, the garden wall and even from the entrance gates went into the new "chimbleys."

On a bluff overlooking the river there was a lovely spot of big pines, carpeted in spring with wild violets, which was the old Negro burial ground. Every Negro who had ever been connected with our family, no matter how far he or she might have wandered, came home to be laid to rest in this ground. Here were buried some of nature's real gentlemen and gentlewomen and some of our truest friends. This graveyard was moved carefully to a high spot close by and in its center stands a granite monument which reads:

To
*the glory of God
and in affectionate
remembrance of all
our people at*
BELVIDERE
PLANTATION
WHO ARE IN GOD'S
SAFE KEEPING, THIS
CEMETERY HAS BEEN GIVEN

by
*Caroline S. Sinkler
Emily W. Roosevelt
Anne W. Fishburne
Caroline S. Lockwood*

JAN. 1941

*"I know that my
Redeemer liveth"*

APPENDIX

Abridged Geneological Table

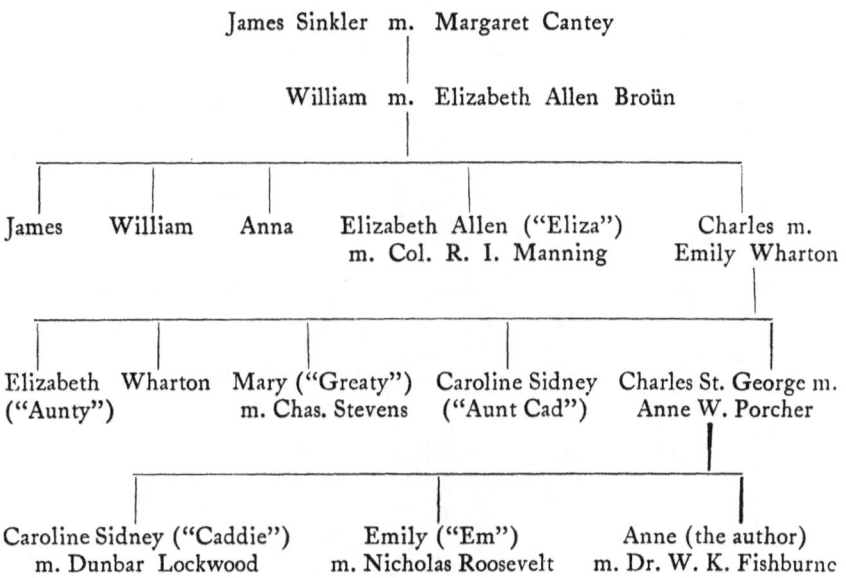

[1] Only persons mentioned in the narrative are included in this table.

www.ingramcontent.com/pod-product-compliance
Lightning Source LLC
Chambersburg PA
CBHW021735220426
43662CB00008B/871